Evaluating Training

Second edition

Peter Bramley has had a long career in training. In the 1960s and 1970s he worked in the Army, first as a trainer and then as organiser of an internal training consultancy for the Directorate of Army Training. In the 1980s and 1990s he discussed issues in training, development and organisational change with MSc and PhD students at Birkbeck College, University of London. He also directed a research and consulting group which worked with many organisations in both public and private sectors on the interface between the development of people and organisational change. He is now retired but still does some writing and part-time teaching.

The Chartered Institute of Personnel and Development is the leading publisher of books and reports for personnel and training professionals, students, and for all those concerned with the effective management and development of people at work. For details of all titles, please contact the Publishing Department:

tel. 020–8263 3387
fax 020–8263 3850
e-mail publish@cipd.co.uk
The catalogue of all CIPD titles can be viewed on the CIPD website:
www.cipd.co.uk/bookstore

Evaluating Training

Second edition

Peter Bramley

Chartered Institute of Personnel and Development

Published by the Chartered Institute of Personnel and Development, CIPD House,
Camp Road, London SW19 4UX

First edition published 1996
This edition published 2003
Reprinted 2004

Design by Pumpkin House, Cambridge
Phototypeset by Intype Libra Ltd, London
Printed in Great Britain by The Cromwell Press, Trowbridge, Wiltshire

ISBN 1-84398-030-4

Chartered Institute of Personnel and Development, CIPD House,
Camp Road, London SW19 4UX
Tel: 020–8971 9000   Fax: 020–8263 3333
E-mail: cipd@cipd.co.uk   Website: www.cipd.co.uk
Incorporated by Royal Charter.   Registered Charity No. 1079797

CONTENTS

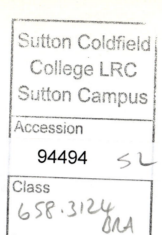

LIST OF FIGURES

LIST OF TABLES

1 ■ INTRODUCTION

Since the first edition of this book was published, interest in evaluation, particularly in the UK, has intensified. The Government has set the tone by requiring the evaluation of virtually everything in the public sector through a variety of forms of target setting and competitive tendering, with the aim of increasing accountability. Organisations in both the public and private sectors have faced increasing demands from customers and regulators to demonstrate achievement of quality rather than efficiency. For instance, it used to be the case that manufacturing in the motor industry was monitored by how many cars were produced per employee per year. Now the criterion is the degree of quality that can be achieved within a price bracket.

These trends are also to be seen within human resource departments in organisations. Training managers are being confronted with sharpened expectations and the requirement to win the training budget against other priorities. In order to win these resources it has become necessary to demonstrate the links between training plans and corporate objectives and then to establish the value of the plans when they are implemented. Evaluation is central to this process and in this edition we look more carefully at how this might be done.

Some traditional areas of training have also changed since the first edition was published. Most of the UK management schools have seen a steep decline in the nominations for public courses and have adapted by increasing the number of tailor-made in-company programmes that offer alternative benefits. Rather more than half of the training in the UK is now delivered 'on-the-job' and should lead to a direct increase in effectiveness. The section on evaluating changes in effectiveness has been expanded to reflect these changes.

There have also been developments in the 'science of training' – the theoretical basis for practice – and these have been reflected in the sections on evaluating changes in learning. Developments in cognitive psychology, social learning theory, the concept of 'self-efficacy' and in theories of transfer of learning have led to a reconsideration of what an ideal process of training might look like. To cover this, a new section on evaluating the training process has been added.

Since the publication of the first edition, the emphases in the literature on training have changed. A major development in the understanding of the training process, which is obvious from the publications of both practitioners and researchers, is that of 'strategic training'. It is, of course, still necessary to maintain the skills pool required to run an organisation efficiently and there is also a need to plan training in support of the immediate business plan. A strategic view implies that there should also be a specific plan for developing skills and knowledge that may be needed in the future and that this should be integrated into the strategic plans of the organisation. Such an approach requires the training manager and other trainers to work much more closely with line managers on aspects of organisational change and the evaluation of 'pay forward' gains in the flexibility of the workforce.

The American Society for Training and Development employs a team that surveys trends in training. The 1997 report (Alliger, Tannenbaum, Bennet et al 1997) isolated a number of trends from surveys of training practitioners in the USA. These included:

- smaller T&D departments, multiple site delivery, internal and external suppliers and outsourcing

- a focus on performance improvement rather than training

- a move towards learning organisations and knowledge management.

Training in the UK also seems to be moving slowly towards this strategic view. The survey carried out for the CIPD in 2000, included responses from senior managers in 600 organisations. Issues that were thought to be 'very important to your organisation over the next two years' included:

- linking training to performance – 75 per cent

- evaluating cost-effective training – 70 per cent

- retention after training – 60 per cent

- containing the cost of training – 60 per cent.

The 2003 report (CIPD 2003) also included information that supports this view that the trend is towards a more business-focused and strategic role for training. In answer to the question, 'When making the case for the training of staff, what is the most important factor?', 80 per cent of respondents said, 'Business issues'. Answers to questions about 'What seems to be changing in the field of training?' included:

- Training is more geared to meet the strategic needs of the business. 92 per cent agreed.

- More bespoke training is being delivered with the aim of solving specific organisational problems. 90 per cent agreed.

Quite a lot of the work involved in this strategic view of training requires the co-operation of others over whom the training department has no executive control. The research on organisational politics suggests that if the department is to have sufficient influence to gain this co-operation, attention to four main areas will be necessary:

- Other departments must really want what training has to offer.

- The activities carried out should be those not easily performed by others inside or outside the organisation.

- The activities carried out should clearly be related to the achievement of high-priority organisational goals.

- The activities should be evaluated and show a positive return on investment.

As with the first edition, this book is written for those people directly involved in training – either as training specialists or as managers who have responsibility for training as a major part of their work. As such, they face demands from all sides for expertise in evaluation. Staff development is only one organisational priority among many and must compete for scarce resources; it needs to be able to demonstrate its value in order to survive and prosper. To reflect this, there is a greater emphasis in this edition on costing training and ideas of cost/benefit.

The aim of the book has not changed; it is to describe techniques that can be used for evaluating training activities. Some of them are simple techniques and some are not so simple. The intention is to describe these techniques and to provide practical advice on how they might be used. If the book is successful in meeting its aim it should be possible for those who wish to evaluate, but have no experience in doing so, to find techniques that they can use and that are appropriate for their purpose.

WHAT IS TRAINING?

We need a definition of the word 'training' to help us think about what we are to evaluate. Training involves learning, but it is rather more than that. Training implies learning to do something and, when it is successful, it results in things being done differently. Much of what people learn during their lives is a result of unplanned experience. Although this can be powerful, it is not a very efficient way of learning. If what is to be learned can be described or specified, then activities can be planned that will facilitate the learning by making it easier and quicker. Training should be like this:

a planned process rather than an accidental one. Within organisations, the investment in training is intended to result in increased effectiveness at work.

The broad definition of training that is developed from these ideas, and is used throughout this book, is

> **❝** a process which is planned to facilitate learning so that people can become more effective in carrying out aspects of their work **❞**

This definition is chosen because it is broad enough to include activities such as on-the-job learning, distance learning, team development, action learning and performance management, as well as courses.

Models of training

Training of individuals has its origin in craft apprenticeships, where a young person learned, over a period of years, to imitate the skills of his master. The learning model here is an ancient one, with hand-eye skills being learned by the method of demonstration, followed by practice, followed by further demonstration. Training for trades and technical training in general have been greatly influenced by this tradition of teaching skills to individuals in the belief that they will later find a use for them. The underlying model is illustrated in Figure 1.1.

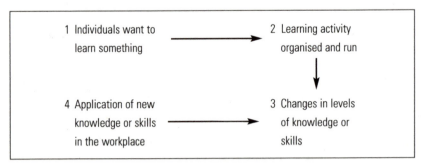

Figure 1.1: a model of training based upon individual education

The focus is on individuals and the process is one of encouraging them to learn something said to be useful, and then expecting them to find uses for the learning. Experience shows that it is often difficult to evaluate training activities based upon this model because changes in work performance seem not to be closely related to the amount learned. What people actually do in organisations is quite closely related to the work context, what is expected of them, and not to how much they know. Thus the model is actually inappropriate where the purpose of the training is to change ways in which work is done. An organisation will have objectives, priorities and policies. It will also have a structure and accepted ways of doing things. All of these situational factors will have some effect on shaping the behaviour of members of the organisation within their work.

The research supports my view, based on experience of evaluating developmental activities, that how much people learn during training is a very poor predictor of what they will do when they return to work ('transfer behaviour'). Written tests of learning predict about 11 per cent of transfer behaviour, and performance tests about 18 per cent (Alliger et al 1997).

Changing the performance of people in the job is much more complicated than Figure 1.1 would suggest. If we are to think about training in support of organisational objectives, what we actually need is a model based upon changing effectiveness rather than one derived from educating individuals. If one were to start at the end of the chain in Figure 1.1, with desired changes in effectiveness, then try to decide what behaviours would be necessary to achieve these, and then analyse what knowledge, skills and attitudes (KSAs) would be required to underpin these behaviours, a model like that in Figure 1.2 would emerge. At stage 4 of this model, aspects of the job situation other than the skills of the people would be considered, and it may be that changing some of these would achieve the desired improvements without training. If training was thought to be necessary it would be delivered and the extent to which any learning was useful would be monitored by changes in job performance, not by changes measured during the training.

This second model for the design of training is much more appropriate for the times in which we live. Most organisations now treat training not as an opportunity for people to learn something, but as an investment that produces returns that can be related to the business plans of the organisation (one of the key questions in 'Investors in People'). This book will show how to build in evaluation at each stage of the design and delivery of training so that this can be achieved.

The book has been planned on the model shown in Figure 1.2. Chapter 2 will cover organisational effectiveness and how to measure it (stages 1 and 2).

Other chapters will describe how to measure changes in behaviour (stage 3), and how to assess learning (stage 4a). In Chapter 7, stages 4b and 5 will be discussed. The intention here is to assist with the decisions about how best to mix training with other organisational interventions in order to facilitate change. A description of methods of evaluating during a learning activity will be found in Chapter 8.

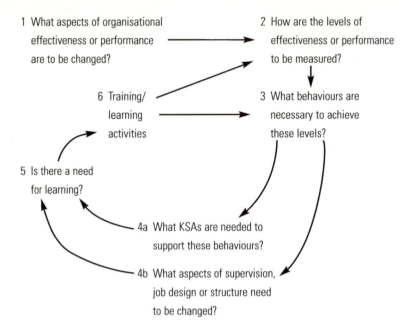

Figure 1.2: a model of training based upon improving effectiveness

WHAT IS EVALUATION?

Evaluation is a process of establishing the worth of something. The 'worth', which means the value, merit or excellence of the thing, is actually someone's opinion. This opinion is usually based upon information, comparisons and experience, and one might expect some consensus in this between informed people. Sometimes there is some disagreement about the worth of something because people are using different criteria to make the evaluation. For instance, some will attribute sentimental value to a piece of jewellery because of its association with a deceased relative, but find that the insurer's value is much lower. The process of evaluation thus provides information about the worth of something, but the decision whether to buy it, keep it, or whatever, may involve values other than those used by the evaluator.

Evaluation of training is a process of gathering information with which to make decisions about training activities. It is important that this is done carefully so that decisions can be based upon sound evidence. Good decisions to introduce, retain or discard particular training activities can make a major contribution to the well-being of the organisation; poor decisions are likely to be expensive. The decisions to be made will need to take into account a number of aspects of the organisational context and future organisational plans, and thus the evaluation process is usually one of providing decision-makers with information, rather than actually making the decisions.

The information gathered may satisfy a number of purposes. It might, for instance, be about the process of training, the changes attributable to it, or increases in the effectiveness of those who have undergone training. It might be to help to decide whether training is the most effective way of achieving some form of organisational change. It should be clear from this that it is necessary to identify the purpose of the evaluation before deciding what information needs to be collected. If this is not done the process of evaluation will lack focus and could become unnecessarily expensive. The aim of an evaluator should be to do a sound job with the resources available; it will never be possible to collect enough information to answer *all* possible questions. Most of the purposes proposed for evaluation can be grouped under three headings:

Feedback   on the effectiveness of the training activities
Control   over the provision of training
Intervention   into the organisational processes that affect training.

Feedback

The most common reason for evaluating training is to provide quality control over the design and delivery of training activities. Feedback to trainers about the effectiveness of particular activities, and the extent to which objectives are being met, will help in the development of the programme being run and in the planning of future ones. What information is necessary for this purpose? You might require:

- some detail about the effectiveness of each learning situation and the extent to which it was suitable for its purpose

- before-and-after measures of levels of knowledge, skills, attitudes or behaviour

- some descriptions of those for whom the activities were of most, and of least, benefit (to define the target population more closely)

- an assessment of the extent to which the objectives set for the programme (by the designers, the participants, the line managers, and the organisation) have been met. These objectives may be set at individual, team, departmental or organisational level.

Feedback evaluation will be of most benefit during the pilot stage of a new programme or when new activities are being introduced into older programmes. It may also be necessary if the target population of trainees changes. The purpose of feedback evaluation is to achieve changes to the planning and delivery of training activities. It therefore follows that the trainers who are to make the changes should be involved in the evaluation. They must feel that the proposed changes are necessary and good if they are to implement them. A fine evaluation report by an independent evaluator, whom the trainers do not trust, could well result in no action being taken. Utilisation of evaluation reports is an interesting area to which we shall return. An excellent reference is Patton (1997).

Control

A second reason for evaluating training is to relate the training policy and practice to organisational goals. There could also be a concern about the value to the organisation of a particular set of activities. Decisions may also need to be made about whether training is the best method of achieving changes. Usually training is not enough on its own, and information about the best way of combining training with other organisational interventions is needed. Decisions may also need to be made about whether a particular set of training activities is worth sponsoring at all.

The information needed for control evaluation is:

- an estimate of the worth to the organisation of the output from the training activities

- an estimate of the cost of providing the activities

- a comparative study of different methods of solving the problem, different combinations of training with other actions such as improving performance management or reallocating responsibilities

- a number of the items listed under Feedback (on page 7)

Control evaluation, if it is to be a relatively objective process, needs a team led by someone who is not the main provider of the activities being evaluated. If the report is to be accepted and used, this person should also be linked to, and respected by, some of the powerful people within the organisation – perhaps the heads of the various interested departments. Control evaluation is almost certain to have some political implications and this should be appreciated when the process of evaluation (including the presentation of the report) is designed. When control evaluation is imposed upon the training department, it may be seen as a threat by some trainers. My view would be that there are advantages to the trainers in this type of evaluation because, if it is properly done, it highlights where training is making a contribution to the well-being of the organisation and where improvements might be made. It is clearly important to the organisation to monitor these criteria.

Intervention

The process of evaluation usually affects the views of people concerned with, or affected by, the training. That a training event is being evaluated will encourage some to think that its future is under review; others may think, 'It must be important, otherwise they wouldn't be spending money on evaluating it.' This can be used constructively by the sensitive evaluator to:

■ encourage the supervisors and line managers to be more closely involved in pre- and post-briefing of participants

■ change the ways in which participants are selected for learning activities so that a greater proportion of those attending are the right people at the right time

■ encourage the co-operation of supervisors in the use of learning contracts and action plans to help integrate training into work procedures and thus ensure transfer of learning

■ facilitate on-the-job activities which complement off-job training and thus foster continuous development.

Evaluation gives a legitimate reason for people from the training department to talk to managers about aspects of organisational effectiveness and how the training provision can assist in increasing this. This is an important political process, which can assist in the liaison between trainers and the line. It can also provide information with which to make decisions about future training plans. Managers are responsible for the development of their staff but many are too willing to devolve this responsibility to trainers. Involving the managers in evaluation shifts some of the responsibility back to the manager and allows the trainer a proper role – as an adviser on developmental activities.

Perhaps you might ask yourself what are the purposes of evaluation in your organisation?

What kinds of evaluation are being carried out?

Do they meet the purposes that you have identified?

WHY EVALUATE TRAINING?

Some of the purposes of evaluation have been described above, but the broader question, 'Why evaluate training at all?' still needs answering. One answer to this question is suggested by surveys of training provision, as these indicate that only 10 to 20 per cent of the learning gained on off-the-job courses result in changes in effectiveness at work (Alliger, Tannenbaum et al 1977: Warr, Allan et al 1999). Can the organisation afford to invest in a wide range of activities that are not making any impact on effectiveness? How will decisions be made about which programmes should run and which should not? Evaluative information is necessary to support these decisions.

Some readers may belong to organisations that are attempting to become 'Investors in People'. Among the questions asked of applicants for membership are:

■ Have you established procedures for evaluating the effectiveness of training in relation to your business needs?

■ Are your line managers and trainees involved in evaluations?

■ Assess levels of increased skills and knowledge: do your evaluations also record whether each trainee's performance on the job has improved?

It is clear that a comprehensive evaluation policy is necessary to answer these questions.

It used to be the case that the contribution of a training department was assessed by the number of days' training carried out during the year, and the value of the department was judged by the number of bids for places. Those days have gone, and with them most of the large training departments offering menus of courses. Now training departments, like other organisational functions, are required to demonstrate how they benefit the organisation. This requires a sophisticated system of evaluation.

There are, of course, costs incurred in evaluating. Sophisticated evaluation by trainers, managers or consultants takes up a great deal of expensive time. However, evaluation can provide clear benefits to be balanced against these costs. These include:

■ improved quality of training activities

■ improved ability of the trainers to relate inputs to outputs

■ better discrimination of training activities between those that are worthy of support and those that should be dropped

■ better integration of training offered and on-the-job development

■ better co-operation between trainers and line managers in the development of staff

■ evidence of the contribution that training and development activities are making to the organisation

■ closer integration of training aims and organisational objectives.

Perhaps the question that we should be asking is not 'Why evaluate training? but 'Can we afford not to evaluate training activities?'

REFERENCES AND FURTHER READING

ALLIGER G.M., TANNENBAUM S.I., BENNET W., et al (1997) 'A meta-analysis of the relations among training criteria'. *Personnel Psychology.* 50, 341–358.

BASSI L.J., CHENEY S. and VAN BUREN, M. (1997) 'Training Industry Trends 1997'. *Training and Development:* November, 46–59.

CIPD (2000) *Training and development in Britain 2000.* London, CIPD.

CIPD (2003) *Training and development 2003.* London, CIPD.

PATTON M.Q. (1997) *Utilization-Focused Evaluation.* Beverley Hills, Sage.

WARR P., ALLAN C. *and* BIRDI K. (1999) 'Predicting three levels of training outcome'. *Journal of Occupational and Organisational Psychology.* 72, 351–375.

2 ■ CHANGES IN EFFECTIVENESS

This chapter describes how stages 1 and 2 in our model of training – the description and measurement of aspects of effectiveness – can be carried out. There is, sadly, no one acceptable definition of organisational effectiveness to help us in this task, and relevant aspects of effectiveness have to be found from the various models on offer. A number of the more useful models will be described and it is hoped that the reader will be able to select one that is appropriate to the particular organisation of interest. It is easy to say that it is important to produce a detailed clarification of what training is trying to achieve in terms of increased effectiveness and so direct the delivery and evaluation. However, this is the most difficult part of evaluation, and, in my experience, this is where most people need help.

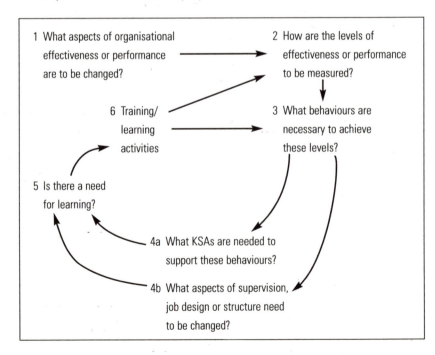

1 What aspects of organisational effectiveness or performance are to be changed?

2 How are the levels of effectiveness or performance to be measured?

6 Training/ learning activities

3 What behaviours are necessary to achieve these levels?

5 Is there a need for learning?

4a What KSAs are needed to support these behaviours?

4b What aspects of supervision, job design or structure need to be changed?

Before doing anything else in planning or evaluating training it is necessary to sort out the *expected impact* that the activities will have on the effectiveness of the whole organisation, or specific parts of it. As with the identification of training needs, the analysis and measurement may be at organisational, team, or individual level. What is being advocated is the production of a detailed statement of how success will be evaluated, in performance measures of individuals, teams or divisions of an organisation, *before* interventions that include training are planned or made. This actually means building the criteria for evaluation into the training objectives.

To some of you, this may seem strange. Many people think that objectives should be set before the event, but that this should be done in a fairly loose fashion to allow for variations in participant requirements. Evaluation is thought of as something that comes afterwards. Evaluation is then a process of asking participants whether the training helped them to achieve the (or their) objectives. My experience as an evaluator indicates that evaluation as an afterthought does not work at all well. If the criteria of success are not carefully described before the intervention starts, the evaluation becomes merely a process of collecting a patchwork of opinions. These will have been affected by the training venue, the particular mix of people on the programme and unrelated organisational changes, as well as by the training intervention. It is much more satisfying – and convincing – to monitor criteria of effectiveness and assess whether they have improved as a result of the intervention.

This chapter repeats, in broad terms, what other books in this series are advocating, that training policy should be closely linked to business plans, organisational objectives and priorities (Boydell and Leary 1996). These should be used as ways of identifying what changes in effectiveness might be desired. When strategic decisions are made about what the organisation intends to be doing in five years time, the implications for staff development should be considered. When training programmes are suggested, a detailed analysis should be made of what benefits they are likely to bring to the organisation. Easy to say, but how can it be done?

Impact analysis

One method of deciding what a programme or intervention should achieve, ie its purposes and how one might evaluate whether these have been achieved, is to carry out an impact analysis.

The starting point of an impact analysis is a workshop in which the *stakeholders* discuss the objectives for the programme and the behaviours that are likely to change as a result of attending it. The word 'stakeholder' refers to the people who have much to gain or lose from the proposed intervention. It will include the trainers who will produce, use or implement the programme and also line managers who are expected to profit in some way from the programme or who may be negatively affected. The intention is to involve a wide range of interested parties and thus get a comprehensive view on the proposed activities. Particularly important will be those who can, if they wish, make it difficult for any changes to take place.

The next stage of the workshop is to ask each stakeholder to write down the three most important purposes of the training intervention as seen from his or her perspective. These statements are collected and pinned up on a board. The stakeholders then clarify the statements as necessary, and group the purposes into clusters. Each cluster is given a title and each stakeholder is asked to allocate 10 points across the clusters. This process leads to a collective view of the main purposes for the programme and their relative importance. Having agreed on a ranking of importance, the group then discusses enabling and inhibiting factors and creates a force-field analysis that shows which factors, including people (both as groups and individuals), might help and which might hinder. Finally, now that the programme has been thoroughly discussed by the interested parties, the stakeholders agree on the best ways of evaluating whether the purposes have been achieved. They may also decide that it is necessary to take benchmark measures at an early stage to allow later comparisons.

The impact workshop may be reconvened some six months after the programme has been implemented, when many of the stakeholders will have a more informed view on it and when it may be necessary to review changes to the programme.

An example of such a workshop (Bramley and Kitson 1994) was the one that set the priorities and means of evaluating them, when it was intended to introduce a number of courses on 'open systems' into a company that produces computer software. Because of the importance of these programmes, and the wide range of people who would attend them, many of the senior managers responsible for the various functions in the organisation were present at the workshop. Some of the key purposes that they set for the programme are listed below:

(1) enable the company to survive and prosper

(2) close a skills gap and facilitate a speedy skills shift

(3) establish a common language

(4) create a desire for more knowledge of the subject

(5) improve management decision-making

(6) create a platform for better business usage of the skills.

The workshop participants discussed this list at some length and made many suggestions for impact measures. These included:

(1) a positive percentage shift in particular business revenue and profit in 'open' products and services

(2) the figure for recruitment versus rationalisation costs; the resourcing of the skills internally; recruit very few from outside and create very few redundancies

(3) the introduction of new training events in the subject; the demand for local delivery of courses

(4) sample key stakeholders and ask them to estimate which business opportunities they have been able to take advantage of directly as a result of having people trained in open systems skills.

The evaluation a year later showed positive results in all of these areas. The estimation of increased opportunities was rather rough and ready, but came to over £10m. This was a very good return on a training investment of £0.6m.

ASPECTS OF ORGANISATIONAL EFFECTIVENESS

Another way to develop criteria against which to evaluate changes is to use some comprehensive framework for categorising aspects organisational effectiveness. One, which I have found very useful, uses four major categories – achieving targets, attracting resources, satisfying interested parties and internal processes (developed from Cameron 1980).

Achieving targets

The most widely used approach to effectiveness focuses on meeting goals and targets. Most organisations use basic measurements of work output to meet *product* goals. The emphasis may be on quality or quantity, variety, uniqueness or innovation, or whatever is the organisational focus. Types of indices that might be available are:

Quantity	Quality	Variety
units produced	defects/failure rate	diversity of product range
tasks completed	reject rates	rationalisation of product range
applications etc processed	error rates	new product/service innovation
backlogs	rework	
turnover	scrap	
units sold	waste	
money collected	shortages	
on-time deliveries	accidents	

An unusual example of increasing effectiveness, where this is defined as meeting targets, was provided by the Lancashire Ambulance Service (National Training Awards 2001). The staff of the LAS serve seven health authorities and a population of 1.4m, many of whom live in remote rural villages. The county's death rate from coronary disease was high, and some of this could be reduced if patients who needed it could receive emergency treatment more quickly. There was no easy way to further reduce the time for ambulances to reach victims, and the solution to achieving the target of lower response times was seen to be to spreading the skills and equipment necessary into the localities.

A commendable money-raising and training programme made this possible, and by the middle of 2001 about 139 members of the public had been trained as 'first responders' to provide 24/7 cover in a dozen communities. The impact of this was a dramatic reduction in response time from a mean of 15.38 minutes for an ambulance to reach an emergency down to a mean time of 5.58 minutes for a first responder. These vital minutes saved lives.

An older but more comprehensive example was provided by NORWEB. Before the privatisation of the electricity supplier NORWEB, an analysis of the organisation's performance showed that the Peak Area trailed behind other parts of the region. It had high revenue costs, high overtime levels and was not meeting NORWEB's guaranteed standards of service. Workshops were introduced in which managers were encouraged to introduce a more consultative management style, and each manager left the workshop with an agreed action plan. Team development workshops for first-line managers and their teams were also introduced. One year later, revenue costs showed a saving of £960k, overtime savings of £500k were made and the Peak Area had achieved all of its guaranteed standards of service. All sickness rate targets were also beaten and this showed a saving of £100k on the year (National Training Awards 1992).

There are also *system* goals, which emphasise growth, profits, modes of functioning, return on investment, etc. Criteria which might be available are:

productivity	rates of achieving deadlines	work stoppages
processing time	output per person/hour	supervisory time
profit	on-time shipments	amount of overtime
operating costs	percentage of quota achieved	lost time
running costs	percentage of tasks incorrectly done	machine downtime
performance/cost ratio	efficiency	frequency of accidents
variability of product or service		

> length of time to train new employees   accident costs
>
> time to bring in new products and services
>
> ability to react to circumstances and cope with external pressures

It is also possible to look at increases in manpower, facilities, assets, sales, etc compared with own past state and with competitors. In public sector organisations, these comparisons often include benchmarking information, performance against key indicators (national and local) and information from 'best value' reviews.

An example of evaluating against system targets was given by one of the major building societies (Bramley 1999). The cost/income ratio was well above the industry average and customer complaints had risen to a level that required a dedicated complaints department. Two-day workshops (which covered process skills, developing staff input of ideas for quality improvement, and team problem-solving) were provided for managers. The effectiveness of these workshops was monitored by systems targets and, after one year, these were considered satisfactory. The cost/income ratio had fallen to the industry average and the level of complaints could be handled by normal line management.

Another example was provided by the Defence Aviation Repair Agency (NTA 2002). Dramatic improvements were needed in the organisation's business performance and productivity if it was to compete successfully. Essentially, a process of establishing and supporting semi-autonomous groups was introduced by training some 300 managers and 400 team co-ordinators over a period of 15 months. This has resulted in improvements in a number of indices of system effectiveness: streamlining the procurement of spares, removal of waste and quality improvements. Turnaround times have also been reduced, some by as much as 35 per cent.

Although the achievement of goals and targets is the most popular method of assessing effectiveness, these are often not the best criteria to be measuring. Goals and targets, set centrally without any real discussion about feasibility, can become sticks with which to beat people rather than measures of effectiveness. This has become obvious in the public sector in the UK. Setting the same targets for all schools has resulted in many of them spending a whole term each year on preparation for the assessment, rather than the teaching of young people. Targets for all hospitals have often resulted in distortions as resources are diverted to reducing waiting lists for one type of treatment in the year of assessment, and then this being neglected because waiting lists for another type of treatment are to be assessed in the next year. Resources are actually chasing the assessments rather than being used in an effective way.

> What measures of 'product' or 'systems' goals are available in your own organisation? Are they being used to derive objectives for training programmes? Could they be used for this purpose?

Attracting resources

Looking at resources changes the emphasis from outputs, goals and targets, to inputs designed to achieve some competitive advantage. At the level of the organisation, the evaluation might be a comparison with major competitors, or against 'how we did last year', or against some ideal desired state. At lower levels, increased flexibility is often the measure that is used. Criteria which might be available for assessing increases in effectiveness include:

increases in number of customers	increase in the pool of trained staff
new branches opened	skills for future job requirements developed
new markets entered	increased flexibility in job deployment developed
takeover of other organisations	readiness to perform some task if asked to do so
ability to change standard operating procedures when necessary	flexibility in meeting changing customer requirements
ability to cope with external changes	improvements in the competence/skills pool

The impact analysis that was described above (p 13) offers an example of improving this kind of effectiveness. One of the criteria used was the number of technical staff recruited (and thus recruiting costs) and the redeployment of present staff (and thus very few redundancies). There are, no doubt, many examples in your own organisation where increased flexibility of staff has resulted in greater efficiency and effectiveness.

Another example of this type of effectiveness is offered by the case study of Toughglass Ltd (National Training Awards 2001). This glass manufacturer faced increasing competitive pressures in its established 'flat glass' market, and in order to secure its future it needed to boost productivity on its existing product and introduce 'curved glass' so as to reach new markets and customers. The company had a reputation for providing predominantly low-skilled factory jobs but needed much more sophisticated processes to manufacture the new product. Workshops were introduced for managers and these addressed issues of obstacles to meeting targets, effective production planning and solving problems. Training was also introduced for the workforce (much of it after shifts, as the company still needed to meet its production targets) as the intention was, as far as possible, to retrain the existing workforce rather than recruit a new one. Increases in efficiency at all levels resulted from these initiatives and new customers were found. There was also an increase in turnover from £5m in 1997 to £11m in 2001.

A further example of increasing effectiveness by entering new markets is given in the case study provided by Hosch GB (National Training Awards 2001). This company was well established in selling scrapers for cleaning conveyor belts to the coal industry. However, as the coal market began to contract during the 1990s the company was forced to look at new markets and customers. Although the product had a very good reputation, it had minimal profile outside of coal and the sales staff had to start from scratch. Because training had been neglected in the years when the company was focused primarily on the coal industry it lacked the skills to sell effectively to new customers. A two-week programme, which addressed the key issues of company and product knowledge, customer service and installation, was custom designed and delivered. Improvements were soon seen across customer service procedures, and gradually new markets were entered and fresh product loyalty was developed. Rather than being heavily dependent on a single major customer, the company now has customers across the power, steel, quarrying, food and other industries. Non-coal sales have been boosted by 300 per cent.

A recent survey of top UK chief executives (carried out by the Institute of Management) found that the primary reason for organisational change was the need to improve competitiveness by reducing costs and increasing the flexibility of the workforce.

Where is the pressure to improve flexibility in your organisation?

What are the implications for training?

Satisfying interested parties

Effectiveness can be judged by the extent to which the organisation meets the expectations of groups whose co-operation is important. Assessment of effectiveness will be against criteria such as the following:

customer complaints	company image surveys
returned material	customer relations surveys
repair orders on guarantee	recall costs
non-receipt of goods	incorrect goods received
product or service quality	meeting statutory requirements
awareness of customer problems	on-time deliveries

Most organisations monitor criteria of this nature but few publish the information. The case of the building society with a high level of customer complaints has already been quoted. Another example is given by the case study of Robinwood (National Training Awards 2001). Here an investment was made in training staff so that they became multiskilled and could play a wider role with customer groups – junior school pupils at an outdoor activity centre. Before the new style training only 30 per cent of the staff could take their groups for all activities and thus build up trust and confidence in the young people. After the introduction of the new training it was possible for 80 per cent to do so. Customer satisfaction levels have increased, the number of re-bookings has increased, and occupancy levels have risen by 20 per cent.

Another example of improving effectiveness by increasing client loyalty is given in the case study offered by the Co-operative Bank Financial Advisers (National Training Awards 2001). The CBFA operates in a very competitive market and was not performing well. Although it was set up to build long-term relationships with clients, it was not attracting repeat business and there was a low level of client loyalty. Sales teams were brought together over a period of four days into workshops using lectures, role-plays and case studies. To make the programme as relevant as possible, sales advisers were encouraged to contribute real life client scenarios as the basis for these case studies. Gradually all of the sales advisers were trained on these workshops and a culture change was achieved. There were many benefits from this, including:

- client loyalty rating increased by 20 per cent

- average sales value increased by 37 per cent

- adviser staff turnover was reduced by 75 per cent

- cost/income ratio was down by 20 per cent

- salesforce was increased by 89 per cent to reflect the growth in business.

Who are the key 'interested parties' for your part of the organisation?

What criteria are they using to evaluate the activities for which you are responsible?

How do they gather the information with which to do this?

Have you any input into this evaluation?

Internal processes

Under this heading, effective organisations are defined as those in which there is little conflict within and between groups, where members feel satisfied with the system and where information flows smoothly. Assessment of effectiveness may be against hard data like turnover of employees, absence, sick leave, etc, but it is often also against surveyed opinions of 'how we were' or 'how we would like to be'. The quality of internal processes can sometimes be assessed by attitude surveys on job satisfaction, group cohesiveness or commitment.

Many survey instruments have been developed by consultants and researchers and useful examples of these inventories can be found in Henerson, Morris et al (1978); Cook, Hepworth et al (1981); Seashore, Lawler et al (1982). Some examples are also included in Chapter 6 of this book, on measuring changes in attitudes. Improvements are usually monitored by comparing percentages of employees who select the 'positive' boxes on scales like: 'agree: tend to agree: tend to disagree: disagree'. For instance, in one of the large building societies the 'positive' percentages to two of the 120 questions on the survey instrument changed as shown below.

	Year 1	Year 2
In my judgement, coy x as a whole is well managed	34%	50%
I would recommend coy x as a good company to work for	41%	51%

The intervention between the year one survey and that in year two, was a series of two-day workshops for managers (Bramley 1999).

Poor quality of internal processes may show in the statistics of:

transfer/turnover	disciplinary actions
absenteeism	grievances
medical visits	stoppages
accident rates	excessive work breakdown

If they are prevalent, such things can be very expensive. The CIPD survey report on labour turnover (CIPD 2002) provides estimates of the cost of one of these indices. An extract from Table 9 in the survey is shown in Table 2.1.

▶ Table 2.1: Estimated total cost of labour turnover per leaver in 2001 by occupational group and industrial sector.

Occupation	Manufacturing	Wholesale and retail trade	Public sector
Managers	£6,410	£4,135	£5,400
Professional	£5,444	£5,185	£4,958
Secretarial and administrative	£2,014	£1,773	£2,712
Craft and skilled manual	£1,900	£1,702	£2,859
Routine unskilled manual	£1,051	£919	£1,125

Can you design a training activity for your organisation which might reduce the incidence of one of these criteria of poor quality of internal processes?

What would it cost?

Would it be worthwhile in cost/benefit terms?

An example of what is possible is given by Cooplands Bakers (National Training Awards 2001). Cooplands was a well-established bakery and retail chain but, despite new premises and facilities, it had high staff turnover and poor morale, and to some extent this was associated with no commitment to training. The company also faced inconsistent quality of product and rising customer complaints. Training was introduced on a part-time, in-house basis and it was supported by performance appraisals. A new pay structure was introduced which reflected skills and NVQ qualifications. The level of staff turnover dropped significantly, and most of the promotions were made internally from the more flexible and multiskilled staff. There has also been a concomitant improvement in the quality of the products, a sharp decline in the number of customer complaints and a marked rise in profitability.

A more detailed example of the value of internal processes was given by the Royal Mail and their use of a survey of employee satisfaction (Bramley 1999). A factor analysis of the questions used in the survey (answered by some 25,000 employees) showed that the crucial aspects of 'satisfaction' broke down into three areas:

From the employer: they wanted job security, fairness of pay, decent conditions of the working environment, fairness of the bonus system.

From their team leader: they wanted to be kept informed, to have realistic targets set, clear direction, notice taken of their views.

Of the team: How well the team worked together, fairness of the system for deciding duties, opportunities to influence decisions, freedom to make decisions.

These areas are ones that could easily be affected by changed management behaviour facilitated by performance management workshops. The question is, 'Is it worthwhile to attempt changes in indices of satisfaction?' or, to put it another way, 'Is there a clear link between employee satisfaction and other indices of organisational performance which can easily be quantified?' The Royal Mail was able to establish that there was such a link by looking at the level of 'satisfaction' in each of the geographical areas and comparing these with indices of effectiveness. Table 2.2 shows the results of this.

▸ Table 2.2: A link between satisfaction and effectiveness

Index of effectiveness	Top 20%	Bottom 20%	Difference
Processing efficiency (%)	74.3	68.6	+5.7
Delivery efficiency (%)	80.6	78.9	+1.7
Sick absence (%)	4.5	5.2	−0.7
Accidents (per 1000 employees per month)	5.0	5.8	−0.8

Those geographical areas that came into the top 20 per cent on the 'satisfaction' measure were better performers on all four key results indices than those that came into the bottom 20 per cent. It was also possible to estimate the value of the differences in the key results indices. Were the Royal Mail to achieve a 1 per cent increase in 'processing efficiency' over the whole country, the estimated saving to the company would be £6m per annum. Similarly, the reduction in costs contingent on an improvement of 1 per cent in 'delivery efficiency' would be £13m pa, and a 1 per cent drop in 'sick absence' would be worth £15m pa. The potential savings associated with higher employee satisfaction are thus enormous.

The CIPD 2003 report showed that the performance indicators that were most frequently used to make a case for training were:

- customer satisfaction (11 per cent)

- business plans (10 per cent)

- organisation key performance indicators (8 per cent).

These are rather imprecise terms and the four categories above of effectiveness, achieving targets, attracting resources, satisfying interested parties and internal processes, should be more precise and particularly helpful when discussing with line managers exactly what is supposed to change as a result of a training programme and how this change is to be measured. It is important, first of all, to establish what criteria the line managers are actually using to assess effectiveness and to identify by what criteria they themselves are being judged. Many of the items under the four categories can be used to clarify these. The next stage is to identify the risks and related costs if these criteria are not achieved. Discussion of this leads to the identification of criteria against which to evaluate the contribution of training activities. To judge from the range of applicants for the annual National Training Awards, it would appear that many private sector organisations are doing this. There is, however, little evidence that organisations in the public sector are doing more than setting unrealistic targets.

You might attempt some mapping of possible changes for courses that are already running using these four categories of organisational effectiveness. Try to identify the intended benefits from a course on something that is generic for individuals at a certain level in the organisation – say principles of management for junior managers – and classify these into the four categories. Try also to classify the intended benefits from another programme which is 'tailor-made' for improving the effectiveness of a particular individual or group at work.

What criteria can you measure?

Which kind of programme do you find easier to evaluate?

If you work within a public sector organisation, can you find criteria of effectiveness against which to evaluate developmental activities?

Can you make the links necessary to provide a case study for the National Training Awards?

Total quality management

It should be obvious to the perceptive reader that the four criteria of organisational effectiveness, discussed above, are interrelated and many of the examples quoted have shown this. For instance, improving the satisfaction of interested parties often implies meeting system targets. Meeting jointly set targets often results in greater motivation and satisfaction of staff and thus is related to levels of turnover, absenteeism and sickness. A more sophisticated model of organisational effectiveness would attempt to show the interrelationships between these four areas. This is the very stuff of total quality management models.

One of the best models on offer is that developed by the European Foundation for Quality Management (EFQM). The nine areas that make up the definition of organisational effectiveness are:

- the *enablers*: leadership, people management, policy and strategy, resources and processes

- the *results*: people satisfaction, customer satisfaction, impact on society and business results.

Some detail on what is implied by seeking effectiveness in these nine areas is given in Table 2.3.

There is a great deal of detail involved in becoming a TQM organisation and the process requires huge changes in the way in which the organisation functions. It is not the purpose here to suggest that any organisation should strive to introduce TQM. The value from our point of view, as evaluators, is the model shown in Table 2.3, which has great strengths. Most attempts at defining organisational effectiveness lead to measures in the 'results' area, some involve 'people satisfaction' and others 'customer satisfaction'. The ISO 9000 has 'processes' as its focus. The great strength of the EFQM model is that it includes all of these and also the 'enablers', without which the results cannot be achieved.

The process being recommended is the use of the EFQM model as an *aid-mémoire* to identify gains in effectiveness which are expected to result from a particular intervention. All nine areas should be examined and questions asked about whether the proposed developmental activities will 'improve ...', or 'fully utilise ...' or 'cause appropriate staff to learn ...' in each of the nine areas. The discussion generated by this should clarify exactly what the intervention is expected to achieve, set targets against which this can be evaluated, focus the design of the learning activities, and identify organisational factors that need attention.

My experience with using this model suggests that, if the intervention is to have a real and measurable impact, at least one area of 'enablers' and one area of 'results' should be included. Where the sponsors are arguing that the intervention will affect all nine areas, it may be so diffuse that the impact is lost because too wide a range of objectives is being set. Some of these objectives may be mutually incompatible, but even where this is not the case, changing all nine areas is an organisational transformation rather than the evolution and development of more effective ways of running the organisation.

An example of the use of a TQM model to set targets and to monitor their

Leadership
- visible involvement of managers as role models, being accessible and communicating
- recognition of the efforts and successes of individuals and teams
- provision of appropriate resources and assistance
- involvement with 'customers' and 'suppliers' both inside and outside the organisation

People management
- continuous improvement achieved by communication with staff
- the skills pool is maintained and developed
- performance management is carried out
- staff are involved in continuous improvement

Policy and strategy
- reflect TQM
- are affected by feedback from staff, customers and suppliers
- are derived from benchmarking against competitors
- are communicated, regularly reviewed and improved

Resources optimised
- financial resources
- material resources
- use of technology
- availability and use made of information

Processes
- critical processes defined and identified
- impact on the business is evaluated
- the organisation manages its processes
- performance measures are used to review processes and set targets for improvement

People satisfaction
The intention here is to satisfy the needs and expectations of all staff by good human relations policies and activities – awareness, involvement, development, reward, job security, health and safety

Customer satisfaction
What the perception of customers (direct and indirect) is of the company and its products and/or services. This should be monitored regularly as it is central to the survival of any organisation

Impact on society
- active involvement in the community
- activities to reduce and prevent nuisance and harm to neighbours
- indirect measures of impact on society, complaints, incidents, etc

Business results
What the organisation is achieving in relation to its planned performance, financial targets, targets and objectives for processes and systems, targets for products, services or market share.

ENABLERS — RESULTS

Table 2.3 The EFQM model of organisational effectiveness

achievement was given by some work in the Post Office Property Holdings group (POPH) (Bramley 1999). This is a small organisation of some 300 people, most of whom are classified as managers. However, it is one of the largest property organisations in the UK, with the role of providing and managing the estate assets to enable the Post Office to achieve its mission. An initial assessment of the performance of the POPH against the nine areas described in the EFQM model showed that it was falling short in three main areas:

1. The achievement of the agreed programme for the year (business results) required improvements in financial performance.

2. The POPH serves other main businesses within the Post Office and a market survey of what they, as customers wanted revealed a low level of satisfaction. Targets were therefore set for improvements in 'customer satisfaction'.

3. A third area where improvement was thought necessary was in 'people satisfaction'.

To improve financial performance, the enabling area is 'optimisation of resources' and some management development programmes were introduced to facilitate this. An examination of the TQM model shows that the 'customer satisfaction' area requires regular discussion with customers to discover what they think to be important and what they think they are not getting. To achieve this, teams were taken out on 'away days' and given feedback on customer opinions, and this led to workshops within the teams to identify key results for themselves vis-à-vis their customers. In order to improve the area of 'people satisfaction', the model suggests that 'people management' needs to be improved. In the POPH this was achieved by cascading team leader training (analysis of leadership skills; purpose/direction/values; action planning) down the organisation and by the introduction of quarterly performance development reviews. The assessment at the end of the year showed improvement in all three areas and that the targets had been met.

THE EFFECTIVENESS OF TEAMS

It is possible to assess effectiveness at a team level rather than that of the organisation (or a department, or function, or section of it). If a team achieves the targets set for it, attracts the necessary resources, or provides products or services which satisfy interested parties, it could be said to be effective, and measures of how effective can be established. It is also quite common to assess the quality of the relationships within the group and how well it co-operates with other groups.

To be called a team, rather than just a group of people who work together, the group must have some common goals and problems. Interdependent action should be required to achieve the goals or solve the problems, and assessment of effectiveness should be based upon the activities of the team rather than those of individuals. If the latter is the case, then it is more relevant to evaluate at the level of individual effectiveness (and reward on an individual rather than a team basis). For instance, a basketball team is a closely knit group, which is highly interdependent even though the individuals in it have different roles. The contribution of an individual is likely to be assessed in terms of how well he or she fitted in and co-operated with other members of the team. A Ryder Cup golf team is actually a set of 12 individuals. Most of the time they play alone and their contribution is judged on how many points they contribute to the overall total. I would not include such a group in the definition of a team.

In work activities there seems to be an increasing tendency to group people into teams in the belief that this will lead to increased effectiveness. Where co-operation is necessary to achieve the desired outcomes this may be sound. The evidence suggests that shared processes like safety at work and customer care become more effective through team development. It is also the case that teams can bring together a wide range of experience, which might be useful in giving different perspectives on the problem to be tackled. Perhaps the strongest argument in support of teamworking is that it is likely to increase participation when change is being discussed. Commitment to objectives, methods, tasks, etc can often be enhanced by participation in discussion about targets and the means of achieving them.

On the other hand, there are many situations where teams are likely to achieve rather less than individuals. The classic study was carried out by a Frenchman in 1913. He asked students to pull as hard as they could on a rope and measured the strength of the pull. They did this individually and then in teams of seven. The average pull of a team of seven was 75 per cent of that of the aggregated individual members' pulls. This has been replicated in many different situations and is generally considered to be an example of 'social loafing', the widespread tendency for people to work less hard in groups than when they are solely responsible and accountable.

Many will argue that groups are more creative than individuals. The research evidence does not support this either. In experiments on 'brainstorming', where people are asked to generate as many ideas as they can (without evaluating whether the ideas are good, bad or silly) in a certain time, a group of five will usually produce about half as many ideas as five individuals in separate rooms. The quality of the ideas produced in the two situations is usually similar. This would suggest that the brainstorming should be done separately and then all of the ideas should be collected. The evaluation of the ideas and selection of those thought worthy of further examination would be better done in the group situation because a range of views and experience would be valuable for this purpose.

Team effectiveness

The literature on team performance and development suggests that there are two main aspects of effectiveness: achieving the tasks set, and longer-term viability through consideration of the well-being of the team members. Some balance between these will be necessary. Too much emphasis on the task can lead to problems with longer-term viability as members are likely to opt out of a situation which ignores their well-being. Great emphasis on well-being can also be dysfunctional as it may lead to a 'cosy' group which spends its time looking inward, talks at length about how difficult life is, and fails to fulfil the organisational purpose for which it exists.

Questions that an evaluator of team effectiveness might ask could include some of those listed below (some of the ideas here have been borrowed from West (1994)).

Achieving objectives

1 How clear are the objectives of the group?
2 How much agreement is there within the group about the objectives?
3 How realistic are the objectives thought to be?
4 What level of commitment to the objectives is there?
5 How concerned are team members with reaching high standards?
6 How often are the objectives reviewed?
7 What feedback is given to the group on progress?
8 How often does the team discuss methods of getting things done?

Well-being

9 Is everyone understood and accepted?
10 Is everyone listened to?
11 Do people support each other when things are difficult?
12 Is conflict brought out into the open and dealt with?
13 Do team members have good relationships with each other?
14 Is there support for new ideas?
15 Do team members help each other to develop?

The questions could be posed in interviews with the team members or printed as a questionnaire. For the latter purpose they might be phrased as statements like, 'The objectives for our team are clear to me' and the team members asked to 'agree/tend to agree/undecided/tend to disagree/disagree' with each statement.

Stakeholders' views on the effectiveness of teams

Another way to assess the effectiveness of a team is to collect the views of those individuals who have an interest in the work of the team. For instance, the important 'stakeholders' may include those who receive goods or services, customers, general management, or leaders of other teams who must co-operate with the team of interest. The team members are also important stakeholders and their views must be considered if the team is to have any longer-term viability.

The opinions that these stakeholders have, about how effective the team is, will reveal which criteria they are using to assess effectiveness and thus provide items for measurement purposes. The framework suggested above (achieving targets, acquiring resources, satisfying constituents and internal processes) should help in this. A list of criteria generated from discussions with stakeholders can be produced and assessed by members of the team. The questions to be asked of each item on this list are:

- 'How important is this?' and

- 'How effective are we at this?'

Where it is agreed that it is important for effectiveness to be improved, other questions can be asked:

- What could we do?

- Who can do something?

- What shall we do?

- Who will do what?

- When shall we review progress?

Developing the effectiveness of teams

Team members need task-work skills to be able to perform individual tasks, and some multiskilling of these is necessary to provide flexibility. Teamwork skills are needed to communicate, interact and co-ordinate tasks effectively with other team members. In general, training should be sequenced so that task-work skills are mastered before teamwork skills are taught (Salas, Burke et al 2002).

The development of teamwork skills may focus on working relationships or on action planning. There are three main models: problem-solving, interpersonal and role-identification.

- The *problem-solving* model encourages the group to identify problem areas that are affecting the achievement of group goals. Action planning is then used as a method of tackling the problems.

■ The *interpersonal* model attempts to improve decision-making and problem-solving by increasing communication and co-operation on the assumption that improving interpersonal skills increases the effectiveness of the team.

■ The *role-identification* model attempts to increase effectiveness by increasing understanding of the interacting roles within the group.

It is, of course, possible to combine the different models, but I find that it helps to think in terms of one or the other when trying to identify criteria against which to evaluate increased effectiveness.

The problem-solving model

There is quite a lot of literature on problem-solving groups, particularly some older work on evaluating the impact of 'quality circles' and the work suggests that this approach can be successful. Members of groups that have worked on their ability to solve problems often report increased job satisfaction, better teamwork within the department, recognition of their achievements, and better relationships with members of management. Management also report benefits, usually that many problems are solved at grass-roots level thus allowing management to concentrate on higher priority items.

It seems likely, then, that the effectiveness of problem-solving groups may be measured in terms of having led to significant cost savings, or having provided possible solutions to the problems identified. It may also be possible to calculate the value to the organisation of solving a particular problem. This might be done directly or by estimating how much expensive consultant time has been saved. Often, team development aimed at improving problem-solving will also improve the quality of working life and feelings of well-being. This would be a worthwhile gain.

The interpersonal skills model

Where team development is undertaken using an interpersonal model, the intention is to increase communication, sharing and trust within the group by discussions on how the members interact with one another.

There is a good deal of published evidence that this kind of activity is likely to have some effect on attitudes – how one feels about others, the workplace, the value of the team, satisfaction with the work. This is the area of effectiveness that we have already seen above as 'internal processes' and it can be argued that improvement in indices of these attitudes would be valuable in themselves as indicators of increased well-being at work. A shared feeling of well-being is likely to contribute towards longer-term viability of the group and it is also possible that improvements in it will be negatively associated with measures of stress, levels of sickness, absenteeism and staff turnover.

Within this sort of approach, it is possible to take measures of other things, before, during, and after the developmental intervention. For instance, an increase in positive responses to questions about clarity of team objectives, amount of information sharing, commitment to excellence and so on, might well be taken as indicators of increased effectiveness.

There is little research evidence to provide a reliable causal link between this kind of team building and improved productivity or achievement of targets. You might think that increased satisfaction should lead to improved performance, but the evidence suggests a flow in the other direction; high performance tends to lead to members of the team being more satisfied and more cohesive (Mullen and Cooper 1994).

The role-identification model

The role-identification model approach treats the group as a set of interacting roles and attempts to increase effectiveness by a better understanding and allocation of these roles. Each member of a team is considered to contribute in two ways: in a *functional* role, drawing on professional and technical knowledge, and in a *team* role, helping the progress of the team towards achieving its objectives. This implies that a team can function effectively only when members recognise and use their team strengths. Observation of groups where three or four people who are outstanding in their field are recruited to form a team indicates that these groups perform in a disappointing way – usually everyone produces ideas and no one wants to develop or apply them. Within any group there should be people who try to get the work done and done on time, as well as those who provide lots of good ideas.

Evaluation of the role clarification approach is difficult because the composition of each group is unique. It should be possible to assess increased awareness of roles, and thus increased openness and willingness to share work, on the part of the group members. However, the links with improved effectiveness in any of the four categories described above are not easy to predict.

Organisational constraints on effective teamwork

Team development activities are attempts to change the way in which the work is done in parts of the organisation. However, if this is to be achieved, some examination of the organisational context in which the team operates will also be required. Poor performance of a team may be due to some aspects of this rather than poor composition, lack of ability, or poor process.

Teams need organisational support in six main areas (Hackman 1990):

1   They need clear goals and targets.

2   Information about present policies and future plans are necessary for a team to integrate its activities with the rest of the organisation.

3   The team needs adequate resources – personnel, financial and administrative support.

4   Training must be provided for team members in areas relevant to their work. Both technical learning and awareness of team processes are implicit in this.

5   Access to technical help should be provided on an 'as required' basis.

6   Regular feedback on performance of the team is necessary.

The organisational context for performance is an important aspect of all training (see stage 4b in our model of training, Figure 1.2 on page 6) and we shall return to this in a later chapter.

What methods are being used in your organisation to increase the effectiveness of teams? How are improvements being monitored? What measures are being taken? A number of different measures have been suggested above; could any of them be used to monitor improvements in team performance?

THE EFFECTIVENESS OF INDIVIDUALS

It is also possible to use stages 1 and 2 of our model of training (Figure 1.2) to decide what changes in the effectiveness of individuals are desired and how these might be measured. Again, it should be clear that the more specific the description of these changes, the more likely it is that training can be designed to achieve them.

Effectiveness is demonstrated in the work context by doing the right things at the right time. It is not just having the knowledge or the right attitudes, although these can clearly be significant contributors to effectiveness. We need to go further than learning, and describe what we mean by effective behaviours.

Key results areas

One way of defining effectiveness in a job is to identify the key results areas. Most jobs have a lot of day-to-day routine activities which need to be done, but have no great impact on whether the job-holder is doing the job well. Key results areas usually represent only a few of the tasks in the job, but are those which are crucial.

There are a number of ways of identifying key results areas, but all require some focusing down to isolate the few *really* important aspects of the job. One method is to list all of the tasks which might be done and then ask the job-holders, and the supervisors, to agree on the 10 per cent that are crucial to success. Another is to start with a long list of possible competence areas, define the job in terms of those that are relevant, and then select from this shorter list (the job definition) the 10 that are key to achievement of the current job objectives. In both of these approaches, it helps for job-holders and supervisors to carry out the analysis separately and then, through discussion, agree the key results areas. More information on how this might be done is included in *Identifying Training Needs* (Boydell and Leary 1996), which is part of this Training Essentials series.

A well-known attempt to list the key results areas for supervisors is given below (Goldstein and Sorcher 1974):

- orientating a new employee

- giving training on-the-job

- motivating a poor performer

- conducting a performance review

- handling discrimination complaints.

For each area, it is necessary to describe the behaviours that are expected to lead to successful performance. For instance, with 'motivating a poor performer', these might be:

- focus on the problem, not on the personality

- ask for his/her help and discuss his/her ideas on how to solve the problem

- come to an agreement on what each of you will do

- plan a specific follow-up date.

Another way of identifying key results areas is to analyse what it is that people who do the job well are doing, and contrast this with the behaviours of people who do not do the job so well. A useful technique for doing this is the repertory grid (described on p 61). For instance, 'repgrid' analysis was used to identify what behaviours were expected from good middle managers (actually section leaders) in an oil company. They were:

- *joint* target setting and reviews of progress
- holding team meetings to *discuss* priorities
- accepting responsibility but *delegating* authority
- asking for views *before* making decisions
- discussing development opportunities with subordinates
- coaching and guiding rather than telling.

The best people to comment on whether managers actually do these things are their subordinates, and further detail on how this information might be collected is given in the next chapter (pp. 42–45).

You may be wondering if there is a difference between what I am calling key results areas and the more general concept of competence. I think that there is. I am not talking about a list of generic competence areas that are required for adequate performance of a job, and which all job-holders will need. These would be provided by some generic training, which would be evaluated on attendance, learning and day-to-day, on-the-job performance. The focus of 'key results' analysis is specific competence areas for particular individuals, which can be improved by some version of just-in-time training and which will have a marked impact on performance.

Individual effectiveness might also be judged by the extent to which targets are achieved. Where action learning is being used, or work-based projects, the achievement of the goals can be related, as a benefit, to the cost of providing the learning opportunities. Learning contracts offer similar possibilities for evaluating against goals, but care is needed to ensure that these lead to increased effectiveness. Where the assessment of the achievement of targets is a rather imprecise appraisal at the end of a year, the process will rarely offer a sufficiently precise focus for evaluation of training activities during the year.

IN BRIEF

Effectiveness is not a simple concept; there are many ways of categorising it, many views on which particular aspects are important, and many methods for defining the criteria of interest. The ones that I have found to be most useful are:

At the *organisational* level

- impact analysis by senior managers

- the four categories of achieving goals, attracting resources, satisfying interested parties and internal processes

- a total quality model like that offered by the EFQM.

At the *team* level

- achieving objectives

- feelings of well-being

- stakeholders' views

- a focus on process issues (we shall return to this in the next chapter).

At the *individual* level

- key results areas.

Many techniques for identifying criteria of effectiveness have been described, but there is also a major underlying theme that I hope has been clearly stated. It is that, although it is difficult to define and measure the criteria of effectiveness that are of interest, it is important to do so.

The criteria that are expected to show an improvement after the training activities need to be identified *before* the learning situations are designed. The activities can then be designed specifically to achieve the desired changes and it will be possible to incorporate any necessary changes in the job context and thus facilitate transfer of the learning. It will also be possible to set up an evaluative framework to discover whether the expected changes have actually been achieved. Trying to identify criteria against which to evaluate as an afterthought, some weeks after the training, is a very poor substitute.

REFERENCES AND FURTHER READING

BOYDELL T. *and* LEARY M. (1996) *Identifying Training Needs*. London, IPD.

BRAMLEY P. (1999) 'Evaluating Effective Management Learning'. *Journal of European Industrial Training. 23,* 3 ,145–153.

BRAMLEY P. *and* KITSON B. (1994) 'Evaluating against business criteria'. *Journal of European Industrial Training.* 18, 1, 10–14.

CAMERON K. (1980) 'Critical questions in assessing organizational effectiveness'. *Organizational Dynamics.* Autumn. 66–80. More fully described in BRAMLEY P. (1996) *Evaluating Effective Training (2nd edn)* Maidenhead, McGraw-Hill.

CIPD (2002) *Labour turnover 2002*. London, CIPD.

CIPD (2003) *Training and Development 2003*. London, CIPD.

COOK J.D., HEPWORTH S.J., WALL T.D. et al (1981) *The Experience of Work*. London, Academic Press

EFQM *Total Quality Management: The European Model for Self-Appraisal*. The European Foundation for Quality Management, Avenue des Pleiades 19, 1200 Brussels, Belgium.

GOLDSTEIN A.P. *and* SORCHER M. (1974) *Changing Supervisor Behavior*. New York, Pergammon Press.

HACKMAN J.R. (ed) (1990) *Groups that work (and those that don't): Conditions for effective teamwork*. San Francisco, Jossey Bass.

HENERSON M.E., MORRIS L.L. *and* FITZGIBBON C.T. (1978) *How to Measure Attitudes*. Beverley Hills, Sage.

MULLEN B. *and* COOPER C. (1994) 'The relation between group cohesiveness and performance: an integration'. *Psychological Bulletin*, 115, 210–227.

National Training Awards 1992, Room W823, Sheffield S1 4PQ. Employment Department.

National Training Awards 2001. www.nationaltrainingawards.com.

National Training Awards 2002. www.nationaltrainingawards.com.

SALAS E., BURKE C.S. *and* CANNON-BOWERS J.A. (2002) 'Tips and guidelines for designing and delivering team training'. In Kraiger (ed) *Creating, implementing and maintaining effective training and development: state-of-the-art lessons for practice*. San Francisco, Jossey-Bass.

SEASHORE S.E., LAWLER E.E., *and* MIRVIS P.H. (1982) *Assessing Organizational Change*. New York, John Wiley & Sons.

WEST M.A. (1994) *Effective teamwork*. London, Routledge.

3 ■ CHANGES IN BEHAVIOUR

In this chapter we shall examine Stage 3 of the training model, attempting to answer the question, 'What behaviours are necessary to achieve increased effectiveness'. Doing this implies being able to:

■ label the behaviours and thus distinguish them from others

■ measure the frequency or quality of the actions that are of interest

■ establish the links with some form of effectiveness.

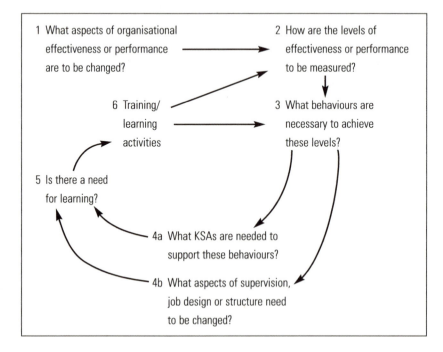

1 What aspects of organisational effectiveness or performance are to be changed?

2 How are the levels of effectiveness or performance to be measured?

6 Training/ learning activities

3 What behaviours are necessary to achieve these levels?

5 Is there a need for learning?

4a What KSAs are needed to support these behaviours?

4b What aspects of supervision, job design or structure need to be changed?

USING A COMPETENCE APPROACH

Probably the best known method of linking behaviours to effectiveness is to list the competence areas that are associated with success. The list may be derived from interviews with, or from checklists filled in by, those who do the work and their managers. Training needs can then be established by assessing individual performance against this list of competence areas. Developmental opportunities, on or off the job, should then be provided in areas of perceived weakness. The training activities to achieve this would be evaluated in terms of whether the learner and his or her manager felt that performance in this area was no longer weak.

The areas of competence required will vary from job to job. The assessment of whether or not there is still a weak level of performance in a particular area can be made realistically only against the requirements of the particular job. Some organisations appear to be attempting assessment of ability on a set of competence areas which *all* should reach to some absolute standards. Chasing high standards in everything, whether or not this is needed, can be very costly in terms of training time and money.

A good example of the competence approach that has survived the test of time is offered by the Management Charter Initiative description of personal competence for managers (MCI). There are four clusters within this – planning, managing others, managing oneself, and using intellect – and each cluster is broken down into dimensions and indicators of desirable behaviour. The framework is given in Table 3.1

For each dimension there are a number of behaviour indicators. For instance, for 'Showing concern for excellence' these are:

- Establish and communicate high expectations of performance. (This includes setting an example to others.)
- Actively seek to do things better.
- Continually strive to identify and minimise barriers to excellence.
- Use change as an opportunity for improvement.

For 'Showing sensitivity to the needs of others' the indicators are:

- Make time to be available to support others.
- Reinforce others' self-worth and value in what they do.
- Demonstrate patience and tolerance when others are expressing themselves or encountering difficulties.
- Demonstrate acceptance of others holding different views.
- Encourage others to express themselves honestly.
- Actively seek to identify and clarify the attitudes, views and feelings of others.

▶ Table 3.1: The MCI Personal Competence Model

Clusters	Dimensions
1 Planning to optimise the achievement of results	1.1 Showing concern for excellence 1.2 Setting and prioritising objectives 1.3 Monitoring and responding to actual against planned activities
2 Managing others to optimise results	2.1 Showing sensitivity to the needs of others 2.2 Relating to others 2.3 Obtaining the commitment of others 2.4 Presenting oneself positively to others
3 Managing oneself to optimise results	3.1 Showing self-confidence and personal drive 3.2 Managing personal emotions and stress 3.3 Managing personal learning and development
4 Using intellect to optimise results	4.1 Collecting and organising information 4.2 Identifying and applying concepts 4.3 Taking decisions

Evaluation will take place by assessing the frequency and appropriateness of use of these behaviour indicators. Measures before and after some feedback and/or developmental activity will indicate whether there has been a change, and if this is in the desired direction.

The strength of this kind of approach is that it breaks down the competence areas into behaviours that can be monitored by the learner, the supervisor, direct reports and colleagues. It is thus possible to communicate whether there have been changes in the desired direction or not.

I would contrast this with the more usual method of using competence areas, within annual performance appraisal schemes. The most common areas are oral communication, leadership, judgement, initiative, organising, written communication, motivation and analytical skills (Hirsch and Bevan 1988). The job-holder is usually judged on areas such as these against a scale of something like 'High/Exceeds/Fulfils/Below' or 'Strong/Adequate/Weak'. It should be clear that these categories are too general and too poorly defined to provide criteria against which to evaluate changes in behaviour and effectiveness due to learning. If this is to be attempted, competence areas should be broken down into the behaviours that are to be used to make the judgements. For instance, with *communication* one might use a set of behaviours such as the following:

- takes time to listen and understand the situation
- chooses the right time to communicate
- chooses the right medium and style for communication
- is assertive and communicates when necessary
- shows sensitivity to the positions and feelings of others.

With *motivation*, a possible set of behaviours might be:

- shows enthusiasm when problems arise
- sees opportunities rather than difficulties
- sets high standards and goes for them
- welcomes responsibility and challenge
- persists when others might give up
- high energy level, can handle a large volume of work.

Below is a specific example taken from a course on 'consulting skills' where some of the behaviours to be learned were related to a category on the annual performance appraisal form – 'interpersonal skills'. The definitions that were used are given in Table 3.2.

▷ Table 3.2 A behaviour scale based upon an appraisal form

Interpersonal skills: usually involves the establishing of sound, straightforward and fruitful relationships with people:

■ the ability to look at a situation from the other person's point of view and balance it against one's own perceptions	Strong/Adequate/Weak
■ the ability to influence others	S/A/W
■ the ability to appreciate how another person feels (empathy)	S/A/W
■ the ability to handle conflict while maintaining a good relationship	S/A/W
■ the ability to convey ideas and agreements with clarity	S/A/W

The behaviours listed were used during the pre-course briefing to communicate to the candidate which behaviours needed improvement and would be targets of the programme. During the programme the participant kept a log of perceived improvements in these areas, and this provided a tracking of attitude change. The format also gave a clear rationale for the employing manager to make pre-and post-training comparisons of behaviour in terms that were well understood within the company. This procedure provided a suitable method for evaluating behaviour change at work.

USING BEHAVIOUR SCALES

These lists of desirable actions suggest a second method of linking behaviours to effectiveness – the use of behaviour scales.

Suppose, for example, that we want to change the management style in our organisation to a more consultative one. We should need to focus on the behaviours shown by middle managers that are consistent with a more consultative style. For instance, we might try to increase the frequency of doing things such as joint target setting and discussing priorities, asking for views before making decisions and delegating authority.

One way of doing this is to define, by listing examples of relevant behaviour, what is meant by the desired approach in the particular organisation of interest, and then assess to what extent these are being shown. For middle managers, the people best able to carry out this assessment are the junior managers who report to them. Some intervention can then be made, based upon feeding back the subordinates' views to the middle managers and then offering opportunities to attend workshops on skills that they then wished to develop. A possible set of behaviours is given below:

1. Jointly sets clear tasks and targets with you

2. Jointly reviews progress on tasks/targets

3. Lets you know exactly what is expected

4. Delegates sufficient authority

5. Is committed to teambuilding

6. Asks for and uses your input

7. Actively supports your ideas

8. Demonstrates concern with development

9. Coaches and guides effectively

10. Shows genuine interest in you and your work.

The subordinates are asked to apply each of the 10 statements to the behaviour of their own departmental head and mark each statement 'agree = 1', or 'tend to agree = 2' and so on, to 'disagree = 5'. For rather obvious reasons this is best done in a way that allows subordinates to give their views anonymously. The opinions can then be collated and used for individual feedback to the managers whose behaviour is being reviewed. Some developmental intervention is then offered and six months or a year on, the process can be repeated and differences noted.

Changes in opinion about specific behaviours are of primary interest and these can be related to the actions undertaken by the departmental heads. It is also possible, by collating all of the results, to gain some information on whether the style within the organisation has changed. For instance, in Table 3.3, the percentages of subordinates choosing the opinions 'agree = 1' to 'disagree = 5' are shown for years one and two of the feedback process (Bramley 1994).

▷ Table 3.3: Comparison of year1/year2 percentages (percentages based on n = 194/193)

	Agree			Disagree	
	1	2	3	4	5
1. Jointly sets targets	10/29	33/43	32/18	23/10	2/0
2. Jointly reviews progress	9/15	22/34	34/21	32/30	3/0
3. Lets you know what's expected	13/20	37/46	20/22	27/12	3/0
4. Delegates sufficient authority	28/45	42/37	16/15	7/3	7/0
5. Is committed to teambuilding	22/38	33/32	28/26	13/3	4/1
6. Asks for and uses input	14/25	36/39	30/27	15/8	5/1
7. Actively supports your ideas	5/16	33/40	44/39	15/4	3/1
8. Demonstrates concern with development	12/21	27/35	27/31	21/11	13/2
9. Coaches and guides effectively	6/15	24/36	37/42	24/7	9/0
10. Shows genuine interest in you and your work	12/29	33/34	32/28	18/7	5/2

The percentages for the first year, on the left in Table 3.3, show that the perceived style was not at all like that defined as consultative. On some of the items less than 50 per cent of the subordinates 'agree' or 'tend to agree' (ie chose ratings 1 or 2) with most of the statements. The percentages in year two are closer to those desired, but still show substantial proportions of subordinates who 'disagree' or 'tend to disagree' (ie chose the ratings 4 or 5). Between the measures taken in year 1 and year 2, the departmental heads learned of subordinates' views on their management styles, discussed these with the consultant and agreed an action plan/learning contract. Opportunities to attend one-day workshops (on joint targetsetting, holding team meetings and developing subordinates) were offered, and many attended them.

The behaviours that showed most change were procedural changes – setting up more team meetings, routine discussion of priorities and progress, putting in place development reviews and so on. Behaviours that were more closely related to personality traits – accepting full responsibility, encouraging new ideas and so on – showed less change.

The Royal Mail also uses this kind of approach to changing management behaviour. Information is collected from employees by using a set of 30 questions about the behaviour of their team leader. The list of questions has six sections – Vision, Commitment, Approach to people, Approach to business performance, Personal contribution of manager, and Communication – which reflect a view of what constitutes effective management behaviour in that particular organisation. In cycle 1, the subordinates are asked whether their team leader does things such as those listed in Table 3.3 (some of these are abbreviated). These anonymous ratings are collated by the team leader, who considers them and then attends a workshop with a group of colleagues. During the workshop, issues are discussed and clarified and options for improvement considered. An outline improvement plan is developed and the leader then meets with his or her team to discuss the implications and actions to be taken. The whole procedure is repeated some six months on (cycle 2).

Statistics are available for ratings by 8,470 team members on the 1,645 team leaders who have been through the two cycles (Bramley 1999). A sample of the questions and the percentages associated with the choices made by subordinates is shown in Table 3.4.

In all of the questions there was a shift to the positive responses of between two and eight percentage points. Given the number of people involved (8,470), these are worthwhile gains. The biggest changes are in questions 2, 12, 15, 17 and 18. As with our earlier example, these items, in the main, reflect changes in procedures. The smallest changes are in questions 13, 23, 24 and 27, and again one sees that these items are largely associated with personal styles and personality variables.

Another way of assessing changes by using behaviour scales is shown in Table 3.5. The categories chosen would, of course, reflect the definition of 'positive management' appropriate to the particular organisation. The perceived frequencies of present use of these behaviours could be assessed by the learner, and objectives set for increased use of some of them. Such behaviour scales also lend themselves to '360-degree appraisal' by seeking opinions of the supervisor, colleagues and subordinates as well as those of the developing manager. Differences in perception between the manager whose performance is being rated and the rest of the set are of particular interest, and these tend to highlight the difference between believing and actually doing something which

▶ Table 3.4: Team members' ratings of leadership behaviour

	Disagree	Agree	Agree strongly
The leader of your team does:	1 & 2	3	4
1 Provide a clear and exciting vision	32/26	55/57	13/17
2 Communicate how the vision translates into stretching goals	34/27	53/57	13/18
7 Involve the team when making decisions	36/30	45/48	19/22
12 Support personal development and training	25/18	49/50	26/32
13 Encourage and value personal feedback	26/22	49/51	25/27
15 Encourage new ideas and suggestions	32/15	50/51	27/34
17 Set high work standards	16/11	51/49	33/40
18 Encourage continuous improvements	20/13	53/54	27/33
23 Display integrity and a caring attitude	23/21	48/50	29/29
24 Walks the job and is approachable	24/21	45/47	31/32
27 Often speaks with the team	22/18	47/47	31/35
28 Asks for ideas and listens	27/21	48/51	25/28
Where: 1=disagree strongly, 2=disagree, 3=agree, 4=agree strongly, 0=not enough evidence to mark			

reflects that belief. This is a common problem in management development, because creating the right attitude does not always result in changes in behaviour in the workplace. We shall look at this in more detail later when we discuss measuring changes in attitudes.

CATEGORISING INTERPERSONAL SKILLS

In some situations, where the cluster of behaviours is not well defined, the first problem is that of being able to describe and label the behaviours that are of interest. One of the first (and still one of the best) sets of categories for doing this is that of Rackham and Morgan (1977). The 13 categories were developed from research on interpersonal skills training. They are defined in Table 3.6.

▶ Table 3.5: A behaviour scale for positive management

Positive Management	Never 0-19	Seldom 20-39	Sometimes 40-59	Generally 60-79	Always 80-100%
1 Thinks ahead and develops plans rather than constantly clearing up problems					
2 Grasps the essential nature of the problem, knows what information is necessary and where/how to get it					
3 Thinks in terms of objectives rather than vague generalisations and makes them both clear and realistic					
4 Takes decisions rather than procrastinating or passing problems up to the next level					
5 Is concerned about, and effective in, obtaining high productivity in the short and longer term					
6 Acts as a model for the group being firm, getting commitment and encouraging participation					
7 Co-ordinates the group's activities and checks on progress to achieve objectives					
8 Deals with subordinates as individuals and makes each accountable for a specific set of responsibilities					
9 Knows what to delegate and has the courage to risk errors by subordinates					
10 Minimises immediate pressure and problems and maximises long-term productivity					
11 Sets high standards and gets them					
12 Knows what is wanted and how to get it without resentment					
13 Seeks increased value for money and year-on-year improvements in efficiency					
14 Rewards outstanding performance					
15 Makes opportunities to develop people as individuals					

▷ Table 3.6: Categories of interpersonal behaviours

Proposing behaviour, which puts forward a new concept, suggestion or course of action (and is actionable)

Building behaviour, which extends or develops a proposal that has been made by another person (and is actionable)

Supporting behaviour, which involves a conscious and direct declaration of support or agreement with another person or his concepts

Disagreeing behaviour, which involves a conscious, direct and reasoned declaration of difference of opinion, or criticism of another person's concepts

Testing understanding behaviour, which seeks to establish whether or not an earlier contribution has been understood

Summarising behaviour, which restates in a compact form, the content of previous discussions or considerations

Seeking information behaviour, which seeks facts, opinions or clarification from another individual or individuals

Giving information behaviour, which offers facts, opinions or clarification to other individuals

Shutting out behaviour, which excludes, or attempts to exclude, another group member (eg interrupting; talking over)

Bringing in behaviour, which is a direct and positive attempt to involve another group member

Defending/attacking behaviour, which attacks another person or defensively strengthens an individual's own position. Defending/attacking behaviours usually involve overt value judgements and often contain emotional overtones

Blocking/difficulty stating behaviour, which places a difficulty or block in the path of a proposal or concept without offering any alternative proposal and without offering a reasoned statement of disagreement. Blocking/difficulty stating behaviour therefore tends to be rather bald, eg 'It won't work', or 'We couldn't possibly accept that'

Open behaviour, which exposes the individual who makes it to risk or loss of status. Included in this category would be admissions of mistakes or inadequacies, provided that these are not made in a defensive manner.

The 13 categories can be used to track the frequency of use of the behaviours that are of interest. Important categories are selected by observing the behaviour of those thought to be good, and contrasting the frequencies used by them with those used by people thought to be less good. For instance, people who are rated as being good at appraisal interviewing:

■ ask more questions, particularly to request proposals or solutions from the person being appraised

■ test understanding more often

- summarise more often

- make fewer proposals themselves.

Another example is that of people who are helping customers choose flights for holidays or business trips. One might expect:

a high rate of:	a lower rate of:	no:
seeking information	proposing	blocking/difficulty stating
testing understanding	giving information	defending/attacking
building	bringing in	shutting out
summarising		

The categories listed in Table 3.6 can be used for on-the-job development by observation and feedback, or for off-the-job courses on interpersonal skills. Their main benefit is that they provide labels so that behaviours of interest can be classified, measured and changed. As we shall see later, the first stage in any skills training is to learn the names of the parts. Without this knowledge, communication about what is required for effective work is very difficult.

BEHAVIOUR IN GROUPS

A good deal of team development work is based upon the view that improving the processes that groups use to work together will increase effectiveness. For instance, having observed a group working together, the facilitator might ask them questions:

- How clear was the purpose of the task? If it wasn't absolutely clear why did you not ask about it?

- Who set the objectives for the meeting? To what extent were these shared?

- Who put in the ideas? Who had ideas that they did not put in? What use was made of creative ideas?

- What actions helped the team? What actions hindered the team?

- How were differences in opinion/difficult issues handled?

The attention is then focused on the processes that are being used, and how effective these are in using the abilities of all members of the team. A useful process model to help with the assessment of this has been suggested by Schein (1987). The framework for the analysis and some of the questions to ask are given below.

	Task	**Interpersonal**
Content	1. Formal agenda, goals	4. Who is doing what to whom
Process	2. How the task is done	5. How members relate to each other, communicate, etc
Structure	3. Recurrent processes, 'standard operating procedures'	6. Recurrent interpersonal relationships, roles

Box 1. Why is the group there? What is its task? What are the goals of the meeting?

Box 2. Do they listen, misunderstand, interrupt? Do they spend time on trivial issues, have side conversations? How is the group chaired? How are decisions made?

Box 3. What procedures are used? Who is allowed to interrupt whom? Have members of the group got particular roles or tasks?

Box 4. Who tries to dominate and control, who argues, who supports whom, who interrupts whom? Who initiates, who checks consensus and who summarises?

Box 5. Do they build on each other or vie for attention? Do they confront each other or are they polite? Is someone persistently attacking someone else?

Box 6. Have they developed a special, common language? Is there a marked 'informal' structure? Are there implicit rules of behaviour? Is there an informal reward system? Are there rituals and procedures for unpredictable events?

The evaluator will note activity in each of these boxes and the key question to consider, in each case, is 'Which of these events are most relevant to increasing the effectiveness of the group?' Feedback to the group and discussion with them should provide some answers to this question.

Research on the role of the team leader suggests that there is also a number of key activities for them. Their behaviour can also be observed and feedback given in the hope of changing some aspects and improving effectiveness. Effective team leaders:

- serve as models for their teams

- openly engage in monitoring, providing and accepting feedback

- provide and accept back-up behaviours

- 'know their stuff' but are willing to listen to other team members who have special expertise

- feel secure and self-confident in their knowledge and ability

- set clear shared objectives

- ensure that specific team tasks are well defined

- allocate roles to team members

- review group processes (McIntyre and Salas 1995: West 1994).

Some aspects of leadership style have been shown to interfere with team effectiveness (McIntyre and Salas 1995). The main problems appear to be:

- micro-management of details

- a tendency towards an autocratic style

- over-confidence with regard to mastery of the technical aspects of team tasks.

These two lists of activities can quite easily be converted into a checklist with which to observe what a team leader does. Concrete feedback on performance can be provided by ticks and crosses against each of these, with a few well-chosen examples to support the opinions. One of the key aspects of team effectiveness is how the team leader behaves, and this observation of process in team meetings offers valuable information on this.

SUMMARY

In this chapter I have tried to show how measures of behaviour can be used in evaluation. In all of the examples the link with effectiveness in the work role has been emphasised. Changing behaviour is not easy, and if it does not result in increased effectiveness the feedback will be unhelpful and the new ways of doing things are likely to be rejected. A model that is worth considering is shown in Figure 3.1. A much more complex and complete version of this relapse process is given in Marx (1982).

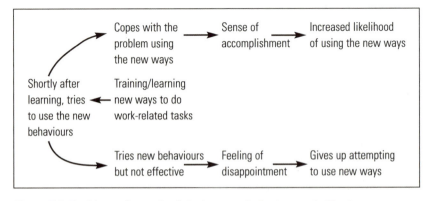

Figure 3.1: Positive and negative links between behaviour and effectiveness.

Effective behaviour is usually context dependent – actions that are successful in some situations are not so in others. The strength of using a competence approach is enhanced when the competence areas identified are those that can be demonstrated in the work setting and are associated with doing the job well. Such categories are ideal for use in evaluating changes due to training interventions. The use of broad, general areas of competence does not provide useful criteria for such purposes.

In assessing whether changes in behaviour have taken place, the opinions of subordinates is particularly valuable. Such information is not often available to managers, and the feedback which it provides can be a powerful stimulus for change.

Behaviour scales need unambiguous, shared definitions. These can be established only by thorough research. It will usually be necessary to spend some time isolating, defining and labelling the behaviours of interest, and then establishing that they have a direct link with effectiveness.

Measures of frequency or quality of the desired behaviours, taken before and after the training activities, will be necessary to establish whether the desired changes have taken place.

REFERENCES AND FURTHER READING

BRAMLEY P. (1994) *Using subordinate appraisals as feedback.* Paper given to the 23rd International Congress of Applied Psychology, Madrid. Copies available from the Department of Organizational Psychology, Birkbeck College, University of London.

BRAMLEY P. (1999) 'Evaluating Effective Management learning'. *Journal of European Industrial Training.* 23, 3, 145–153.

HIRSCH W. *and* BEVAN S. (1988) *What makes a manager? In search of a language for management skills.* University of Sussex, Institute of Manpower Studies.

MARX R.D. (1982) 'Relapse prevention for managerial training'. *Academy of Management Review.* 7, 27–40.

MCI Pocket Directory, Middle Management Standards (1992). London, Management Charter Initiative.

McINTYRE, R. M. *and* SALAS E. (1995) 'Measuring and managing team performance'. In R.A. Guzzo, E Salas and Associates *Team Effectiveness and Decision Making in Organisations*, Wiley.

RACKHAM N. *and* MORGAN T. (1977) *Behavioural Analysis in Training.* Maidenhead, McGraw-Hill.

SCHEIN E.H. (1987) *Process Consultation Volume II*. Reading, Massachusetts, Addison Wesley OD Series.

WEST, M.A. (1994) *Effective Teamwork*, London, BPS and Routledge.

4 ■ EVALUATION OF LEARNING: CHANGES IN KNOWLEDGE

In this chapter, and the two that follow, techniques for measuring learning will be described and discussed. In our model of training this represents stage 4a, 'What knowledge, skills and attitudes are needed to support these behaviours?'

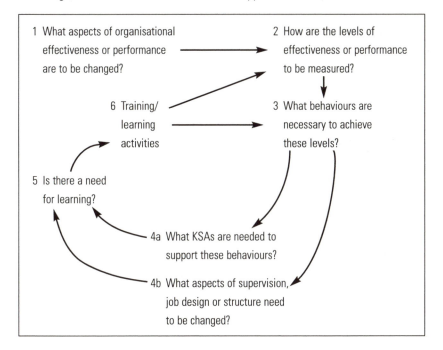

1 What aspects of organisational effectiveness or performance are to be changed?

2 How are the levels of effectiveness or performance to be measured?

6 Training/learning activities

3 What behaviours are necessary to achieve these levels?

5 Is there a need for learning?

4a What KSAs are needed to support these behaviours?

4b What aspects of supervision, job design or structure need to be changed?

There is an interesting debate about when learning can be said to have taken place. Some psychologists would argue that learning is a relatively permanent change in behaviour, and thus that learning in an organisational context can be demonstrated only by changes in the ways in which work activities are carried out. Others would argue than learning takes place when people begin to think differently. Learning can then be an end in itself, regardless of whether it results in different work behaviours. The debate is interesting because it forces one to think about the underlying model of training. The model based upon technical education (Figure 1.1, p 4) has, as its third stage, 'changes in levels of knowledge or skills' and the fourth stage, whether or not these are applied, remains an assumption. When using this model, the effect of the training would be evaluated by assessing whether learning has taken place. Training as a process of increasing effectiveness (the model shown above and in Figure 1.2), assumes that learning is required to produce changes in work behaviour. A more appropriate level at which to evaluate learning would thus be that of assessing changes in behaviour.

Whichever model is being used, it is possible to specify what learning is required for satisfactory job performance, measure the level before a training activity and again afterwards, and thus evaluate whether the expected learning has taken place. Learning is a 'whole person' activity and it has knowledge, skills and attitudinal components but, to achieve some clarity in presentation, techniques for measuring aspects of learning will be described in the following three chapters.

CHANGES IN KNOWLEDGE

Almost all of the tasks within a job require the job-holder to have some knowledge. One aspect of designing a training activity would, therefore, be to:

- discover what knowledge is required for satisfactory job performance

- discover what trainees know when they start the training

- plan how best to facilitate the closing of this gap.

A method of clarifying what knowledge is required that I have found valuable is to carry out an analysis at three levels of complexity (Bloom 1956):

Level 1, facts: the basic requirement for knowing facts, rules and lists. This is often called *declarative* knowledge; information about 'what'. For instance, a counter clerk at the Post Office would need to know what forms have to be filled in and what documents produced in order to apply for a vehicle licence disc.

Level 2, procedures: knowledge of procedures, how things are done, how to order sets of actions. This *procedural* knowledge implies information about 'how'. For instance, starting up a processing plant involves a series of actions which must be done in a certain sequence.

Level 3, analysis: being able to recognise the key features in particular situations and thus select the most appropriate procedure from a number of possibilities. This is often called *strategic* knowledge; information about 'which', 'when' and 'why'. For instance, a social worker might have to decide whether a youngster's needs are best met by leaving her in the family of origin or by taking her into care, either by fostering or in a residential home.

If a preliminary needs assessment identifies level 3 activity as an important job skill, subsequent task analysis can specify the types of problem most frequently encountered and discover whether it is important to be able to identify problems, generate possible solutions or evaluate potential solutions (Kraiger 2002). This should, of course, affect the accuracy of the simulation of job situations required to provide a realistic preparation.

The three levels are built on each other in increasing complexity and the training should be designed to move up the levels. The training needs analysis will be at all three levels to facilitate this design process. The evaluation might be at any level, but will usually be a demonstration of ability at levels 2 or 3. The present trend away from classroom training will make this more difficult. The ASTD report in 1999 (Bassi and van Buren 1999) predicted that companies would reduce classroom training by 20 per cent between 1997 and 2000, replacing it with various forms of computer-based training. The CIPD 2003 report also picks up on this trend to increase the use of new technology. The percentages claiming to use the method for some of their training have increased:

	2002	*2003*
Intranet	25.5%	52.2%
Extranet	9.8%	21.6%
Internet	26.4%	47.7%

Such learning packages are often very efficient at facilitating learning at levels 1 and 2 and testing of the learning can be built into the package. However, they are not good at facilitating learning at level 3, and one fears that this may be left to casual on-the-job supervision – one of the least effective ways of learning. The motivation for the use of new technology is often that it will reduce the costs of instructors, travel, etc, and thus prove less expensive and more convenient, but experience has shown that this is usually not the case (Whalen and Wright 2000). This is an important issue and we shall return to it in Chapter 7 on evaluating before the event.

Measuring knowledge

Testing of knowledge is common in technical education, in trade testing and when candidates apply for membership of professional bodies. Those who do not have the required level of knowledge are thought not to be able to do the work. This ought also to apply to in-company training, but often it does not. This is usually because the analysis of needs has not been done in sufficient detail to justify statements like, 'The level of knowledge that X has shown implies that he or she should not be given work of type W'. There is, of course, a great deal of sensitivity about testing ability, particularly that of managers, and one needs to be on firm ground in order to make such statements.

Open-ended questions which require short answers can be asked to assess knowledge of facts, lists and procedures. They can also be used to test powers of analysis. The answer expected should be short, and a clear statement of how long the answer should be and how it should be laid out, should be given. Examples of this kind of question are:

Briefly state three reasons . . .

List the five most important . . .

It is relatively easy to write questions of this type to measure trainees' knowledge of a particular topic. The marking of the answers may, however, pose some problems. Answers may vary but still be correct, so it is necessary for the person marking the answers to be a subject expert and this may be an expensive use of such a person's time. If there is more than one marker there will be problems of reliability of the marking, and a detailed marking guide will be necessary.

Objective test items

An alternative to open-ended questions is to use *objective test items*. This means asking the learners to write one or two words, or select the correct alternative from a number offered. With these objective test items the rules for scoring are made absolutely clear so that the answer can be recognised as being right or wrong and can be marked so by someone who knows nothing about the subject area being tested.

Objective test items have the advantage over open-ended questions in that they take less time to answer and the test can therefore cover a much wider area of the topic in the same time. They are also less likely to be testing the level of literacy of the candidates. They have the disadvantage of being rather more difficult to write.

The most popular format for objective tests is to use a stem and four or five alternative responses, for example:

A tachometer is used to indicate:	a Road speed
	b Oil pressure
	c Engine speed
	d Distance travelled

The person being tested circles or ticks the alternative selected. The answers should be clearly right or wrong so that anyone with a marking guide can decide whether the answer is correct or not. The marking then becomes a simple clerical task rather than one for a subject expert.

Simple guidelines are available for writing this kind of test item. For instance:

- The stems should:
  - be clear and brief
  - not include negatives
  - not give clues by using key words which are repeated in the correct answer.

- Incorrect alternatives (usually called distracters) should be plausible and arranged in a random order so that the correct answer cannot be guessed because of its place in the sequence of alternatives.

- The items should be grouped by type so that the instructions can be made simple.

There is a belief that objective test items are suitable for assessing only levels 1 and 2 in our hierarchy of knowledge. This is not necessarily the case. The Open University, for instance, does a lot of course assessment by using objective tests and some of the items are not testing recognition of simple facts. An example is the sort of question where understanding of a theory is being tested by asking which of a set of statements is consistent with the theory. Some of these questions test the ability to apply the theory in new situations, a procedure which is at the third, analytical, level of knowledge.

Objective test items are sometimes difficult to write because a sufficient number of plausible alternatives cannot be found. In this case, it is possible to use a specific form, the true/false item, for instance:

Road signs which are triangles with red borders are warning signs

True/False

With this type of item it is necessary to avoid the use of words like 'never' or 'always' in the stem as these are usually false statements and thus offer help in identifying the correct answer.

It is clear that if a person who knows nothing is faced with a true/false test, he or she will score about 50 per cent by guessing at each item. A guessing correction can be applied to calculate the actual level of knowledge:

True score = Number of items correct – Number of items wrong

With multichoice items there is less likelihood of guessing in a random fashion. If necessary, guessing can be reduced by requesting that the candidates should not guess but leave questions unanswered when they have no idea what the answer is. It is also possible to use a guessing correction, with the formula now becoming:

$$\text{True score} = \text{Number right} - \frac{\text{Number wrong}}{(\text{Number of alternatives} - 1)}$$

For instance, a candidate has 75 right, 15 wrong and has not attempted 10 on a multichoice test with four alternatives.

$$\text{True score} = 75 - \frac{15}{(4-1)} = 75 - 5$$
$$\text{True score} = 70$$

As the candidate has not attempted 10 of the questions, can one say that she guessed the answers to the 15 that are wrong and five that are right? I think probably not; it seems more likely that the candidate had some idea about these answers, otherwise she would not have attempted them. The amount of guessing that is occurring can, in itself, be an interesting measure of knowledge. Someone who has learned something and who is answering questions, should not need to guess.

Test results contain a good deal of information which can be of use in evaluating training. The mean (or average) mark tells us something about how difficult the test was for the trainees. Comparison of two sets of scores from different groups of trainees will give an indication of whether one group learned more than the other. However, test results should be taken only as indications until the test has been established as a reliable instrument. The procedures for doing this can be quite complex, but a simple way to check on reliability is described in Appendix 1. Further information can be found in Bramley (1996).

Gains in knowledge

If it is intended to attribute changes in levels of knowledge to training it would appear to be logical to measure knowledge before as well as after training and thus estimate the gain. Testing only afterwards is risky as it may be that some of the participants actually know more before training than they do afterwards. You think that is a ridiculous statement? Well I know of an occasion when it happened. I was asked to help with the evaluation of a knowledge-based programme – the learning of product knowledge to support sales of particular products. The information to be learned was nicely packaged and an assumption was made that all of the sales staff should work through the packages and complete the knowledge tests. I suggested that they should be pre-tested as well as post-tested, and this was done. We found that some of the experienced sales staff scored higher marks on the pre-test than on the post-test! They had either been confused or bored by the learning packages.

When the learners can be considered to know very little and they can safely be given a pre-test score of zero, pre-testing is a waste of everyone's time. Sometimes it is worthwhile calculating the gain in knowledge during the programme to measure the efficiency of the training medium. A ratio can be calculated by using the formula:

$$\text{Gain ratio} = \frac{\text{Post-test score} - \text{Pre-test score}}{\text{Possible score} - \text{Pre-test score}} \times 100\%$$

This ratio represents how effective the programme was for a particular individual, ie whether the trainee learned 50 or 70 or 90 per cent of the information that he or she did not know. An average gain ratio can be calculated for a group of trainees, and this will give an estimate of how efficient the training method was for that particular group. Some methods are more effective than others, probably because of the amount of *active* learning involved, and one should expect something like:

30 per cent with short lectures followed by questions
50 per cent with a good instructor and a good balance between input and practice
70 per cent or better with individualised instruction of programmed packages.

Following up knowledge-based programmes

I would argue that the knowledge learned should be necessary for some aspect of the job. Therefore, the evaluation of knowledge gain is not complete until the trainee has been followed back into the workplace to discover to what extent the knowledge is useful. This can be done by questionnaire, and a suggested format is given in Table 4.1.

▶ Table 4.1: A questionnaire for following up knowledge-based programmes

Topic (A detailed list of the areas covered on the programme)	How useful is knowledge of this for your job?	Have you used knowledge in this area since the course?	Have you had any difficulty in applying this?
	Very/Quite/Not	Often/Seldom/Never	No/At first/Still
Topic 1			
Topic 2			
Topic 3			
etc			

Where more than a third of people who return the questionnaire do not think that the knowledge is useful, or have not used it in six months following the training, the relevance of the topic should be reviewed. This is best done by interviewing a sample of people doing the job, and their supervisors.

Where people say that they 'still have difficulty' they should be asked to specify, as far as they can, what is the nature of the difficulty on the open spaces printed on the back of the questionnaire form. It may be necessary, when these are examined, to seek further information about the precise nature of the difficulty. Again, this is easiest to do in interviews.

A fourth area might be investigated on the front of the questionnaire by asking, against relevant topics, whether the reference material supplied was adequate. Sometimes, if good written material is prepared for courses, the trainees can use this to help them after training and, where this is possible, the time spent on the topic during training can be reduced. It would certainly be worthwhile asking them if this was the case. Places on off-the-job training are limited and expensive.

MENTAL MAPS

Assessment of knowledge at the third, analytic, level implies finding out how the learners are recognising the key features in the situation and how they are making decisions about which procedures might be appropriate. This will often mean asking trainees about their level of awareness and understanding in order to estimate how they are organizing the knowledge that they have. For instance: asking them how they are making decisions about which procedures are more likely to succeed; asking them about what sub-goals they have for the procedures they intend to use; and how these link to the overall goal of solving the problem.

Sometimes the concepts that people have are confused and it is necessary to find out how they are thinking about the topic by carrying out an analysis of their 'mental maps'. A useful method for this analysis is the *repertory grid*. Using this technique, the investigator asks the learners to consider a number of situations and to say what criteria he or she would use to distinguish between them, usually to distinguish those that went well from those that did not. This is often done in interviews, but it can be done with groups and, for our purposes of evaluation, the group method will usually be more practical and less time-consuming. An example of the group method should help to clarify the procedure.

Suppose you are planning a programme for junior managers on 'communication'. A good starting point would be to try to discover what they think good communication skills are. It should then be possible to plan the programme to start from this baseline and, by building on this, move their views closer to those that are thought valuable within the organisation.

You start by asking the participants to write down the names of six managers with whom they have worked, two of whom are thought to be very good communicators, two of whom are thought to be poor, and two who are in between. Each participant does this separately. No attempt is made by the tutors to explain what they mean by good communication skills as the intention is to find out what the *participants* think. Each name is then written on a small piece of paper, these are shuffled and then coded A, B, C, D, E and F.

You now ask them to select A, B, and C from the six and think about what these three might do in work situations where they are required to communicate. What is it that two of them might do that is similar? What is it that one might do that the other two would probably not? Each of the participants selects a pair from the three labelled A, B and C, who are likely to behave in a similar way and a single who would behave quite differently. Each then writes down the pair description on the left of a prepared form, as below:

Triad Selection		
Pair	**A B C D E F**	**Single**
Description	* * *	**Description**
Try to make sure that I understand		Too busy, just tells me

Quite often these are obviously opposite statements, but this is not always the case.

Next they draw the managers D, E, and F from the six and repeat the process of deciding what two of them would do that makes their behaviour alike, and what the other one would do that would be different. For instance:

Triad Selection							
Pair	**A**	**B**	**C**	**D**	**E**	**F**	**Single**
Description			* * *				**Description**
Listen to what I have to say							Not interested in my views

It is important to supervise this and to ensure that the descriptions that are being written down are about what managers *do* rather than descriptions of personality. Quite often the trainees will want to write down things like, 'warm personality', but statements like this are at too high a level of generality to help us decide what needs to be learned in order to demonstrate 'warmth'.

The procedure is repeated until they have written down a number of contrasts by comparing different combinations of managers. Drawing three from the six in 10 ways, say ABC, DEF, ACF, BDE, ADF, BEF, CDF, ABE, BCD, ACE, will ensure that each manager is entered into the comparisons six times. If different behaviours are described each time, this should give enough information on how each participant thinks about ways of communicating.

The next stage is to relate these contrasts to judgements about what the participants think represents good practice. This can be done by a simple scoring process. On each line, the participants score their contrasts on a one to six scale by giving the manager who is most like the pair description a 1, and the one who is most like the single description a 6. Then 2 and 5 are allocated to the next most like, and so on with 3 and 4. For instance, if manager C is most likely to seek assurance of understanding and manager A is always too busy you might have:

Pair	**A**	**B**	**C**	**D**	**E**	**F**	**Single**
Description							**Description**
try to make sure that I understand	6	2	1	3	4	5	Too busy, just tells me

If manager D is best at listening and manager F is not interested, you might have:

	A	**B**	**C**	**D**	**E**	**F**	
				* * *			
Listen to what I have to say	5	3	2	1	4	6	Not interested in my views

Some of your participants might want to use shared rankings (equal 3, etc) but they should not be allowed to do this.

When they have scored all 10 contrasts, these scores can be correlated with their view of good communication skills. This is done by each of them ranking the six managers who make up the A to F using 1 for the best communicator and 6 for the worst. These numbers are written down on a separate piece of paper, say:

Overall	A	B	C	D	E	F
Effectiveness	6	3	2	1	4	5

The ranking on overall effectiveness is now correlated with that on each of the contrasts, for example:

Pair	A	B	C	D	E	F		Single
Seek understanding	6	2	1	3	4	5		Too busy
Overall	6	3	2	1	4	5		
Differences	0	1	1	2	0	0	= 4	

Pair	A	B	C	D	E	F		Single
Listen	5	3	2	1	4	6		Not interested
Overall	6	3	2	1	4	5		
Differences	1	0	0	0	0	1	= 2	

The differences in ranks are summed, regardless of sign, to give a score. The direction of the signs, plus or minus, does not matter; it is the size of the difference that is important. Where the score for the difference is small, ie 0 or 2, the description of behaviour that is being contrasted is very close to what the participant understands by good communication skills. Because of the method of scoring, you will get a high score when the positive description is on the right (ie the single description). Thus the highest possible scores (18 and 16) also show what the participant means by good communication with the positive example on the right. (It is usually worth checking the arithmetic at this stage. There are six pairs and therefore all of the scores should be even numbers; those people who have odd numbers should recalculate the differences).

Contrasts that have scores of between 4 and 12 will be ways in which the participants think that managers differ. They are not, however, closely related to what they understand by good communication skills.

The contrasts that have scored 0 or 2 or 16 or 18 can be discussed with individual participants to draw out what, for each of them, is the definition of good communication skills. With a group, these contrasts can be collected and written up on flip charts. This provides an interesting way to introduce the programme.

For instance, at the beginning of a five-day programme of trainer training, one of our groups produced a list that included the following:

Most effective trainers	Least effective trainers
Confident in subject	Not interested
Ability to simplify	Inability to simplify
Can use different styles	Simply teaches
Outgoing	Laborious
Pitches talk at audience	Arrogant
Clarity of communication	Difficult to understand
Well prepared	Disorganised

Some personality descriptions have slipped in here and these contrasts need further expansion. What was meant by 'outgoing' and what behaviour would be classified as 'arrogant'? These are questions that would need to be asked. Discussing types of behaviour like this gives a good lead into talking about what good trainers do and thus into the main topic for the programme.

This group procedure takes about one-and-a-half hours, but it gives a good feel for the understanding that the participants have at the beginning of the programme. It is also a good introduction to the area as it requires them to think carefully about the subject and clarifies what they, as individuals, believe.

Towards the end of the training the procedure above can be repeated, and the results compared. As they will now be familiar with the process, the second attempt will take much less time – perhaps 45 minutes. Changes can be assessed in a number of ways:

- More contrasts scoring 0 or 2 or 16 or 18. At the beginning many of them will have only a few such contrasts as their views about the topic are likely to be rather woolly. At the end they should be much more focused on the area that has been discussed.

- There should be fewer personality traits and more descriptions of what people do.

- The constructs being used at the end should be influenced by what has been included in the programme.

The evaluation of a course for sales staff offers an example of a before-and-after analysis of constructs (Honey 1979). At the beginning of the training, the delegates produced constructs like the following:

Effective sales reps	Least effective sales reps
Good sales records – gets results	Doesn't turn in good results
Highly self-confident	Less assertive
Ambitious	Unimpressive
Sets clear objectives	Plays things by ear

Towards the end of the programme, their understanding had changed and they were thinking more about behaviours than about personalities. They produced contrasts like:

Effective sales reps	Less effective sales reps
Listen as much as they talk	Talk far more than they listen
Modify their behaviour in interaction	Stick rigidly to a predetermined plan
Use a genuine problem-solving approach	Use an 'I am here to sell you something' approach
Use a range of different approaches/styles	Fixed characteristic style

The repertory grid is a sophisticated technique, with many variations to suit particular situations. Perhaps the most common use is to define what behaviours are associated with success in a particular organisation. The behaviours or competences that distinguish between successful and less successful senior managers can provide a basis for management appraisal and for development through assessment centres. An example of the product of this process is the behaviour checklist in Table 3.5 (page 46). Another common use of rep-grids is in customer service training, for identifying suitable and unsuitable behaviours when dealing with customers.

An interesting example of the use of 'rep-grid' analysis in the public sector was reported by an investigator into the fostering process (Nissim 1999). Children who can no longer live with their family of origin may be looked after in another family, by foster parents. The investigator was exploring how to improve the quality of placement of the children in foster families. One aspect involved asking the main interested parties what they understood by the expression, 'a good fostering placement'. The interested parties were the foster parents (carers), the children, the social workers who are responsible for particular children, and the family placement social workers who are responsible for finding foster families. A 'rep-grid' was used and a number of interesting issues became apparent.

The *carers*, when asked to produce contrasts that distinguished between successful and less successful placements, produced a list of characteristics of the children, things like:

Wanted to be part of the family	Rejected my family and me
Rational and approachable	Lack of social skills
Clean and tidy	Tells lies
Well-behaved	Argumentative, unreasonable

Of particular interest was the fact that they did not produce *any* contrasts that described the actions of *carers*. In other words, they did not see their own behaviour as being important to the success or failure of the placement.

The social workers for the children produced a list of characteristics of carers, things like:

Handle behaviour problems well	Not enough understanding
Set and stick with firm boundaries	Overly high expectations of child
'Stickability'	Lack of commitment
Sensitive	Unimaginative

They also produced a few characteristics of the children, but *none* of them wrote down any description of their own behaviour, as the social worker responsible for the child. Again, they did not see *their* behaviour as contributing to the success or failure of the placement.

The family placement social workers, who are furthest removed from actual cases, produced much the most complex picture. They showed that their understanding of the process included a wide range of carer characteristics, a lot of information about the types of youngster, some constructs about the family of origin and some about the efforts of social workers.

The value in using the 'rep-grid' was that it revealed that there was a good deal of variation in the way in which the groups of interested parties thought about fostering. This was important both for the design of workshops to improve the quality of fostering, and for changes in organisational procedures.

▌ IN BRIEF

The level of knowledge that people have is relatively easy to assess. Measurement at level 1, *facts*, can be carried out by using open-ended, short answer questions or objective tests. The latter are used more often than the former because they allow more questions to be asked in a given time and thus a wider coverage of the knowledge.

Measurement at level 2, *procedures,* can be carried out using objective test items, but is more often done with open-ended, short answer questions. Listing the steps, or 'what would you do next' questions require the learner to *recall* the knowledge, whereas objective test items often prompt the learner by offering a set of alternatives from which the correct answer is to be *recognised.*

Measurement at level 3, *analysis,* often implies asking the learners about their mental maps, how they are making decisions about what to look for, how they decide what to do next, and so on. The repertory grid can be useful in clarifying some aspects of this because it requires the production of the contrasts that are being used to make judgements.

Knowledge tests are not so widely used as one might imagine. They are common where it is necessary to demonstrate that professional standards have been reached. They are also common in packaged instructional material that is based upon the format of 'test, then learn, then retest'. This self-appraisal of level of knowledge is good learning design as it provides clear goals for the learning and feedback on performance. Goal-setting helps with both direction and persistence of learning (Locke and Latham 1990) and is thus a useful motivator.

REFERENCES AND FURTHER READING

BASSI L.J. *and* van BUREN M.E. (1999) *The 1999 ASTD State of the Industry Report.* American Society for Training and Development.

BLOOM B.S. (ed) (1956) *Taxonomy of Educational Objectives.* London, Longmans.

BRAMLEY P. (1996) *Evaluating Effectiveness Training.* (2nd edn). Maidenhead, McGraw-Hill.

CIPD (2003) *Training and Development 2003.* London, CIPD.

HONEY P. (1979) 'The repertory grid in action'. *Industrial and Commercial Training.* September.

KRAIGER K. (2002) 'Decision-based evaluation'. In Kraiger (ed) *Creating, implementing and maintaining effective training and development.* San Francisco, Jossey-Bass.

LOCKE E.A. *and* LATHAM G. P. (1990) *A Theory of Goal-setting and Task Performance.* Englewood Cliffs NJ, Prentice-Hall.

NISSIM R.E. (1999) *Substitute Family Placement.* Unpublished doctoral thesis. University of Reading.

WHALEN T. *and* WRIGHT D. (2000) *The business case for web-based training.* Norwood, Mass, Artech House.

5 ■ EVALUATION OF LEARNING: CHANGES IN SKILLS

In order to answer the question, 'What skills are necessary to support effective behaviour?' some form of analysis will be required. This should identify key skills and the level at which they are required for satisfactory job performance. To clarify what level of skill is necessary, it is helpful to have a set of levels to assist in the planning of assessments before, during and after learning. A suggested set of levels is given below:

- The basic level with skills is the ability to label things, to identify parts, etc. Without this it is very difficult to learn how to do things differently. Assessment of skill at this level is, essentially, a knowledge test.

- The second level is that of performing simple procedures, often with the use of instructions or notes. By simple procedures I mean things like changing the wheel on a car, where there is a sequence to follow and each part of the procedure involves a simple skill.

- A third level is that of performing skilled actions. These often require considerable practice. For instance, planing a piece of timber to the required size, or typing at 70 words a minute.

- A higher level of skill is that involved in judging whether a piece of skilled work is of acceptable quality. For instance, judging a sequence of driving manoeuvres to decide whether or not a driving licence should be awarded. Assessment of skill at this level is time-consuming and quite difficult as the testing situation will require the person being tested to make correct decisions on a number of examples.

The level of skill required for satisfactory job performance is the benchmark, but training will not always achieve this level. It is common for people who have just finished training to be carefully supervised until they achieve the level required of an experienced person. An understanding of the gap between the level that is likely to be achieved in training and that required for experienced performance should be shared between those designing the training and the employing manager. The latter will often want high levels of performance, which cannot be achieved economically in off-the-job training. The use of the four levels above, with assessment of what the trainee can do at each level, should help to clarify differences in expectation and the requirement for further practice.

Skills at level 2 can be learned fairly easily, and practice can be supported by check-sheets until the skills become well established. Knowledge of the procedure might not be sufficient without some attempt at performance to increase the likelihood of retention. For instance, like many others, I tend to ignore the demonstration of how to fit a life jacket, which is offered at the beginning of most flights. Simple though this procedure is, I do sometimes wonder how many would actually be able to tie the jacket on correctly, should that become necessary. I am sure that if they were required to do it, just once in their lives, there would be a much greater likelihood of satisfactory performance (Kraiger 2002).

Level 2 skills may be taught off-the-job if using the actual equipment is likely to be dangerous or too expensive. Often such skills are learned on-the-job by 'shadowing' an experienced person. Sometimes this is not the best way to learn because experienced operators tend to use shortcuts and some of them take risks. If this is likely to be the case, on-the-job trainers should be selected and given some training. For instance, policemen and women who are undergoing their probationer training learn many of the skills on the job by going on patrol with an experienced constable. It has been found that these tutor constables need careful selection and some training if they are not to teach the probationers their own bad habits.

Skills at level 3 will often be practised to the level where they become automatic. For instance, in the early stages of learning to drive a motor car, the learner will need complete concentration to let in the clutch, change gear and pull away smoothly. Later, it must be possible to do this automatically, so that some attention can be paid to the conditions of the road and traffic movements. This 'skill automaticity' is required in many tasks so that attention can be given to making decisions rather than being glued to the detail of the process. The implication of this is that, before planning training activities, it will often be necessary to decide which parts of the skill need to become automatic (Schraagen, Chipman et al 2000). These aspects should be 'overlearned' and a good deal of practice will be necessary, some of it after mastery has been demonstrated. Care is needed in this analysis as overlearned skills are difficult to change. For instance, having spent many years driving a car with a manual gear shift most drivers find it difficult to drive a car with an automatic gearbox. The problem is that, when approaching a corner, the left foot 'automatically' seeks the clutch pedal and hits the foot brake. One feels rather foolish driving while sitting on the left foot, but something drastic may have to be done to overcome the learned automaticity.

TESTING SKILLS

Skills should usually be tested by practical tests. Sometimes it is possible to assess the skill by asking the candidate to state the correct sequence of actions. However, listing the sequence is often not the same as actually performing the task. I can explain to someone how to set the make/break contacts in the distributor on my old tractor, but when I *do* it I never seem to get the setting right.

Tests of skills fall into two main types:

- The trainee is set a task (for example to repair something) and the work is inspected at the end of the test period.

- The trainee is watched throughout the test so that the methods used can be assessed.

Inspecting finished work is a more economical use of the tester's time than watching the whole process but, if the actual procedure is important, it may be necessary to spend the time doing this. Some kinds of welding, for instance, need to be watched during the process as the quality of weld will not be obvious from a simple surface inspection.

Where long procedures are being tested, watching the whole process allows the possibility of correcting the trainees who make mistakes early. They may then carry on with the test rather than stop, and have the possibility of showing that they understand other parts of the procedure.

Research into the use of assessment centres has shown that practical tests, based upon job tasks, are better predictors of job success than knowledge tests. This is probably because they more accurately simulate the tasks for which people are being trained. Practical tests do, however, have some disadvantages:

- They are expensive to supervise.

- They often tie up expensive equipment.

- It is also difficult to screen candidates so that they cannot see what others are doing.

They can also be unreliable if a detailed marking guide is not used. Just how serious this can be is demonstrated by a simple exercise using electrical three-pin plugs. Six plugs are wired up to three-core cable with one wired correctly and the others with defects, say:

a wired correctly	d wrong lead to earth
b live lead to neutral	e loose cable retainer bar
c too much bare wire	f one loose connection

A number of people are asked to mark the finished work (and given no further information). Usually people will mark the wired plugs out of 10 and some will give quite high marks for work that is actually dangerous. In later discussion, it can be established that some aspects of the work are critical because they involve safety. Then it becomes obvious that candidates who ignore safety aspects must fail. The general point being made here is that, where more than one marker is being used, some standardisation of the marking guide will be necessary to ensure reliability of testing. A guide will also be needed for the observation of performance tests. Standard driving test schedules are made up of lists of critical skills, each to be performed to a satisfactory level. For other performance tests it might be possible to video-record a few attempts at the skill and, from these recordings, develop a marking schedule. Figure 5.1 shows a simple schedule (for marking attempts to change a car wheel) that was developed by this method.

Another example of a schedule for assessing skilled performance is given in Table 5.1. Here the intention is to observe a tutor and then use the categories on the schedule for feedback to improve future performance.

With skills training there is often an assumption that the learners know very little and that pre-testing is, therefore, inappropriate. This is not always the case. Sometimes pre-testing will show that the training programme needs to be modified to meet different target populations, some of whom know nothing and some needing only a little extra training.

One method of doing this is to use a 'trainability test' (Downs 1977). The essential components of the skill to be learned are analysed and then tasks are constructed which will incorporate some of these. The tasks must:

- be based upon crucial elements of the job

- use only such skills as can be learned during a brief learning period

- be sufficiently complicated to allow a range of observable errors to be made

- be capable of being carried out within a reasonable time.

	Tick as applicable	
Serial sub-tasks	YES	NO
1 Stop on hard, level surface		
2 Apply handbrake	*	
3 Engage low gear	*	
4 Chocks of bricks in front and behind wheels	*	
5 Remove tools and spare wheel		
6 Check tyre pressure of spare and adjust if necessary		
7 Place jack under chasis nearest to wheel to be changed		
8 Loosen wheel nuts		
9 Jack up wheel approximately 1" from ground		
10 Remove nuts – top nut last		
11 Remove wheel		
12 Place spare wheel on hub		
13 Secure top nut first	*	
14 Tighten all nuts, diagonally	*	
15 Lower jack – wheel on ground		
16 Tighten nuts fully	*	
17 Place spare wheel in carrier		
18 Clean tools		
19 Replace tools		
20 Question student on subsequent check (nuts to be checked at next inspection)		
* These are critical tasks as they involve safety, and failure to observe them will result in a failure of the test.	Result PASS/FAIL	

Figure 5.1: Changing a wheel: marking schedule

A trained tester, normally an instructor who is experienced in the job, demonstrates what has to be done, or briefly teaches what has to be learned. The applicant then tries to complete the task under test conditions observed by the tester. A record is made of errors made during this part of the process.

▸ Table 5.1: A performance schedule for a taught lesson

'Put X in the box if you feel that some improvement can be made. Write down a comment for each X so that the feedback is precise and describes something specific.'		
Signposting	**X**	**Comments**
Introduction		
Statement of objectives		
Outline of stages		
Summaries at stages		
Delivery		
Eye contact		
Use of voice		
Use of questions		
Checking understanding		
Control		
Time allocation		
Good pace		
Kept to subject		
Use of aids		
Contribution		
Variety		
Overall Impression		
Knowledge		
Enthusiasm		
Created interest		
Mannerisms		

A trainability test of this type was used in the selection of applicants for the job of machinist (Downs, Farr et al 1978). The candidates were graded on the test as:

A = extremely good – would expect her to become a very good machinist in a short time

B = fairly good – would expect her to reach 100 per cent performance in a reasonable time

C = Good enough for simple work — would expect her to become a steady worker on a simple machine or task

D = Would have difficulty in training

E = Would not be trainable.

One great strength of this procedure is that it can assist in the redeployment and training of staff at a time when skills are becoming obsolete and new skills need to be learned. This is now a common experience, and it is worth while trying to avoid the costs of losing good staff and the recruiting costs of replacing them. The survey on labour turnover published by the CIPD in 2002 estimated the cost of turnover per leaver in the 'operative and assembly manual' category, as £1,663. Training costs can be reduced by establishing that the proposed trainees can easily learn the skills necessary. It is also the case that realistic job samples allow the potential trainees to make an appraisal of whether they actually wish to do that kind of work; motivation is always an important aspect of learning.

Another reason for pre-testing is to try to 'tailor' the programme to those who need training. Some years ago, I was asked to help with the training of fitters to carry out servicing of central heating systems in homes. An off-job programme of three one-week modules was designed to cover the skills necessary to carry out the work. All the fitters were tested using fault-finding exercises mounted on boards that represented the main types of heating system. The ways in which the fitters attempted these simple diagnostic tests were used to decide how many of the one-week modules each should attend. It was then possible to plan a programme of training courses which accurately met the skills needs across the population of fitters. Really efficient training is made possible by assessing the starting level of the trainees and then offering just-in-time learning.

PROFILING SKILLS

Profiling is widely used in education as a method of recording the development of students. In technical education the best known example is that of City and Guilds of London, which uses a format of five attainment levels, each of them defined. For instance, the levels for 'planning' are:

1	2	3	4	5
Can identify the sequence of steps in everyday tasks with prompting	Can describe the sequence of steps in a routine task after demonstration	Can choose from given alternatives the best way of tackling a task	Can modify/extend given plans/routines to meet changed circumstances	Can create new plans/routines from scratch

These definitions are taken as benchmarks, and a discussion takes place between the learner and the tutor about which category best describes the present level. Sometimes testing will be used to identify this level. One of the levels is identified as the next objective, and a learning programme is put in place to achieve the change. A date is agreed at which progress will be reviewed. The strength in this benchmarking is that it makes the objectives of the learning explicit and thus identifies targets for the learner. This is a motivational device, which is very powerful in encouraging learning because agreed goals and priorities are set for the learner.

Following up skills-based programmes

Technical skills that have been properly learned transfer easily to the workplace. The reason for following up skills training is not so much to check on transfer as to ensure that the training time is being used effectively, ie to train those skills that are actually required and to train them only to the level necessary. The principal task is to check that the original needs analysis was correct. The questions that need answering include:

- Could they have easily learned the skill on the job?

- Do they do it often enough to make it worthwhile training everybody on it?

- Are the levels right or do they need further development on the job?

- Is that part of the job still done in that way or are the trainers out of date?

Follow-up questionnaires of the type in Table 5.2 will provide most of the information

Table 5.2: A follow-up questionnaire for skills based courses

Tasks	How often?	Is it difficult?*
Since the course have you had to:	Never Sometimes Often	Never At first Still
Diagnose mechanical faults in . . .		
Repair or assist the repair of . . .		
Use . . .		
Supervise someone using . . .		
etc. . .		
* If it is still difficult please specify the reasons in the blank spaces on the back of this page.		

necessary. These should be sent to the participants some time after training when they have had some opportunity to experience the range of the job, usually between three months and a year, depending upon the complexity of the work.

When following up skills training it will almost certainly be necessary to contact the supervisors or employing managers, and this can also be done using a questionnaire. Something like that in Table 5.3 should prove useful.

▶ Table 5.3: A follow-up questionnaire for supervisors

Tasks	Is it necessary for him/her to do this?	Can he/she do it to your satisfaction?	Would you rather have trained him/her to do this yourself?
The trainee has been taught to . . .	Yes No	Yes without supervision Yes with supervision	Yes No
Diagnose mechanical faults in . . .			
Repair or assist the repair of . . .			
use . . .			
Supervise someone using . . .			
etc . . .			

It may be necessary to interview a sample of participants and their managers to discuss details of why things are difficult or why some performances are not up to standard. This might be done directly or by telephone.

▌IN BRIEF

The testing of skills has been common practice for a very long time. The classic model for skills learning is:

- instructor demonstrates the whole task

- instructor breaks down the task into stages and demonstrates these one by one

- learners practise the stages one by one

- learners connect the stages to carry out the whole task

- learners are tested for proficiency.

The testing can be carried out relatively informally but, if it is to be reliable, quite detailed marking schedules may be needed. These should include critical aspects that need to be carried out correctly or safely if the performance is to be judged satisfactory.

An important aspect of the evaluation of skills training is the assessment of whether the skill is actually necessary for successful job performance. It is also worth considering whether the learning of the necessary skills is best done on the job or off. Key criteria to help with this decision might be:

- the availability of on-the-job supervision and coaching

- the time to proficient performance

- the possible risk to people and equipment of on-the-job training

- the cost of off-the-job training.

Some of the skills needed by managers might be assessed in the ways described in this chapter or by testing their knowledge. However, most of their learning is intended to change the ways in which they do things in the work context and it is usually more informative to assess the learning at the behavioural level. As we have seen, it is also possible to assess their learning by some measurement of the effectiveness of the team or section or department for which they are responsible.

REFERENCES AND FURTHER READING

CIPD (2002) *Labour Turnover 2002. Survey Report.* October, London: CIPD.

DOWNS S. (1977) *Trainability testing: A practical approach to selection training.* Information Paper no ii. London, HMSO.

DOWNS S., FARR R.M. *and* COLBECK I. (1978) 'Self-appraisal: A convergence of selection and guidance'. *Journal of Occupational Psychology*, 51, 271–278.

KRAIGER K. (2002) 'Decision-based evaluation'. In Kraiger (ed) *Creating, implementing and maintaining effective training and development.* San Francisco, Jossey-Bass.

SCHRAAGEN J.M., CHIPMAN S.F. *and* SHALIN V.L. (2000) *Cognitive Task Analysis.* NJ, Erlbaum.

6 ■ EVALUATION OF LEARNING: CHANGES IN ATTITUDES

One of the effects of learning is that the attitudes of the learners tend to change. They may become more interested (or less) in the topic being learned and, in some cases, become determined to carry on learning more about it. They may become more confident in their ability to carry out job tasks. They may become more convinced that the organisation in which they work is interested in their development and that it offers opportunities for personal growth. These changes in attitude are usually not the only aspects of learning that are of interest to an evaluator, but it is possible to assess them and it is sometimes valuable to do so.

It is important to be clear about what is being measured when assessing people's attitudes. An attitude may well be a predisposition to behave in certain ways, but it does not imply that a person *will* do what is expected. For instance, after a short course on assertive behaviour, the participants may say that they intend to behave in a more assertive way when they return to the workplace. Whether they actually do so depends to a great extent upon the reactions of others. People are social animals and they tend to behave in ways that they believe to be appropriate to the situation in which they find themselves.

▌MEASURING ATTITUDES

When we are measuring attitudes we are collecting evidence of feelings, values and beliefs. These may change from time to time for reasons that are outside the control either of the person trying to assess them or the person whose attitudes are being assessed. Aspects of the situation affect the thing being measured. For instance, at the end of short off-the-job courses, most trainers collect the reactions of the delegates to the content and process of the learning activities. When the food, the accommodation and the sports facilities have been good, the attitudes will be much more positive than when these have been poor. What does this tell you about their views on the content and process of the learning activities?

So we need to be careful about what we are measuring and what conclusions are being drawn. One way of deciding what to measure is to think about attitude change as a means of moving people along a continuum. Take a series of steps like those below:

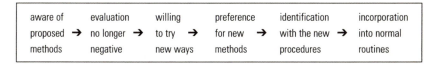

aware of	evaluation	willing	preference	identification	incorporation
proposed →	no longer →	to try →	for new →	with the new →	into normal
methods	negative	new ways	methods	procedures	routines

Assess where they are at the moment and then find some way of moving them a few steps to the right. It is possible to keep asking questions of people to discover where they are on this continuum, before, during and after learning activities, which are intended to achieve knowledge and skills changes. Their attitudes are likely to be as important as their abilities in predicting what they will do and what they will not do after training.

Self-confidence and self-efficacy

Another way of expressing this is to say that what we are trying to do is increase their self-confidence. A general increase in self-confidence is a tall order and takes a good deal of time, but it is realistic to try to increase their confidence to tackle specific tasks. This rather narrower attitude – the perception that a particular task can be carried out successfully – is called 'self-efficacy' in the psychological literature (Bandura 1986). It has attracted a good deal of attention because it has been shown to be a good predictor of the amount of learning during training and a very good predictor of work-related performance (Stajkovic and Luthhans 1998; Thayer and Teachout 1995).

Self-efficacy is measured by asking for self-assessments of confidence to do particular tasks. For instance:

In order to reduce the frequency of system 'crashes' on my PC, I can find the 'Normal' file (which contains the underlying logic) within Word 2000, delete it and have the system construct a new Normal file free from unwanted contamination. I am capable of doing this:

	Can do yes/no	If yes, confidence on a scale of 1 to 10 (not at all – totally)
1. on my own	_____	_____
2. when I am provided with written instructional material	_____	_____
3. when I am able to listen to someone giving instructions who pauses while I complete each step	_____	_____
4. when I am able to watch someone going through the steps before I try it myself	_____	_____

Another example, which was actually used in a piece of research, involved the measurement of confidence to do particular aspects of the job of first-line manager before, during and after an outdoor activity programme (Donnison 1993). The managers were asked:

How would you rate your confidence to carry out the following tasks and be successful in doing so? (Not at all confident = 1, Absolutely confident = 10)	
Items like the following were used:	
Motivate and encourage staff to achieve goals	_____
Monitor the performance of staff	_____
Make decisions on work-related issues	_____
Maintaining standards and quality of work	_____
Managing your own time	_____

The measures used showed an improvement in the managers' self-efficacy after the programme, particularly for those who were low at the beginning. Some of this increased confidence was transferred back to the work situation and resulted in greater effectiveness.

The development of self-efficacy is an important aspect of the training process, and we shall return to it in Chapter 8.

Semantic differentials

A simple way of measuring attitudes, and thus monitoring changes, is to use pairs of antonyms – words that have opposite meanings. At the beginning of the workshop, the participants are asked to think about a particular topic and to express their view on it using seven-point scales. For instance, one that I have found useful when running workshops on 'evaluating training' is shown in Table 6.1.

▶ **Table 6.1: A semantic differential**

Evaluation of training is:								
Valuable	1	2	3	4	5	6	7	Worthless
Sincere	1	2	3	4	5	6	7	Insincere
Relevant	1	2	3	4	5	6	7	Irrelevant
Objective	1	2	3	4	5	6	7	Subjective
Fair	1	2	3	4	5	6	7	Unfair
Fast	1	2	3	4	5	6	7	Slow

The opinions of the group can be summarised at the beginning of the workshop as frequencies on each line by counting those choosing a particular number. Some discussion then takes place about why the numbers have been chosen and this starts to identify attitudes to the topic. The exercise can be repeated near the end of the programme and any changes in attitude can be identified. It should be possible from this to assess whether positive changes have occurred on the dimensions of interest.

Other pairs of words that might be suitable for other topics are:

good–bad	friendly–unfriendly	strong–weak
interesting–boring	clear–confusing	profound–superficial
open–closed	relaxed–tense	useful–useless

It is, of course, possible to be more specific about the contrasts in which you are interested. For instance, with a workshop on evaluating training, you might start with opposites like those in Table 6.2.

The questions represent important issues that need to be discussed and resolved within the workshop. The process of filling in, and then discussing, such an attitude measure raises awareness of these issues and starts the attitude changes that seem to be necessary.

▶ **Table 6.2: Views on the process of evaluation**

Evaluation of training *should* be:		
Statistical and scientific, as its primary concern is with objective measurement	1 2 3 4 5 6 7	Anecdotal and descriptive, as its primary concern is with subjective interpretation
A carefully planned process with a set agenda	1 2 3 4 5 6 7	Changing throughout as the focus changes during the process
Estimating the worth of training activities to the organisation	1 2 3 4 5 6 7	Providing feedback to the training department
Based on large samples and asking quite simple questions	1 2 3 4 5 6 7	Based on small samples and using in-depth questioning
Part of the process for all training activities	1 2 3 4 5 6 7	Carried out only when there is some doubt about a programme
(Adapted from an idea by Len Gill, of Merseyside Police)		

ATTITUDE SURVEYS

Surveys of opinions on issues thought to be important to the effectiveness of the organisation have already been mentioned in Chapter 2, when we considered 'internal processes' as one method of assessing effectiveness. Such surveys are used by many organisations to monitor year-on-year changes in the attitudes of employees, and some of the items can be used to provide information for the evaluation of training activities.

Two types of format are widely used. One is based upon antonyms like those above, and an example is shown in Table 6.3.

It should be possible to use questions like those in Table 6.3 to monitor changes in attitudes of employees. To some extent these could be affected after the introduction of management workshops on 'team development', 'delegating authority and responsibility', and so on. They could also be affected by other changes in the work situation which have nothing to do with training; for instance, changes in rates of pay or decisions on 'downsizing' the organisation.

▷ Table 6.3: An example of a format for an attitude survey

Please fill in the inventory below by circling the number that you think best describes your part of the organisation.		
The management:		
is task-centred and impersonal	1 2 3 4 5 6 7	people-centred and caring
is cold, formal and reserved	1 2 3 4 5 6 7	warm, informal, friendly
emphasises conserving resources	1 2 3 4 5 6 7	emphasises developing and using resources
Decisions are:		
made by 'legal mechanisms'	1 2 3 4 5 6 7	made by problem-solving
treated as final	1 2 3 4 5 6 7	can be altered as circumstances require
made at the top	1 2 3 4 5 6 7	made at the lowest possible level

Another way of laying out an attitude survey of this type is to label the statements 'x' and 'y' and ask whether the respondents agree with one or the other. An example of this is shown in Table 6.4.

▷ Table 6.4: An alternative layout for assessing attitudes using paired statements

Statement X	AX	TAX	U	TAY	AY	Statement Y
Communication in this organisation passes down, top to bottom						Communication flows across and upwards, as well as down
People hide what they really think and feel						People tend to express what they think and feel
(AX=Agree X, TAX=Tend to agree X, U=Uncertain, TAY=Tend to agree Y, AY=agree Y)						

An alternative format, which is often used in surveys of attitudes, is to offer only one statement and then ask whether or not the respondents agree with it. An example is given in Table 6.5.

Some prefer 'strongly agree/agree' and 'disagree/strongly disagree' to 'agree/tend to agree' and I think this is simply a matter of preference. Some designers of attitude surveys wish to force an opinion by not including an 'uncertain' column. I am dubious of the value of this. I have found that my main interest has been in the strength of

▸ **Table 6.5: An alternative format for an attitude survey using single statements**

	D	TD	U	TA	A
1. When developing a new policy, away days are held so that all interested parties can discuss the issues.	1	2	3	4	5
2. Action plans from performance appraisal discussions influence the development of policies.	1	2	3	4	5
3. When there is conflict you can expect a way forward to be imposed from above.	5	4	3	2	1
4. The management develops policies, we are informed of the details and expected to implement them.	5	4	3	2	1
5. Policies are strongly influenced by interested parties outside of the organisation.	1	2	3	4	5
6. When there is conflict you can expect differences to be aired, and support in finding a way forward.	1	2	3	4	5
(D = disagree, TD = tend to disagree, U = uncertain, TA = tend to agree, A = agree)					

'positive' responses of TA and A, or the 'negative' responses of TD and D. The use of an undecided column helps with the assessment of this. If your decision is to use only four columns, I would suggest that you use a fifth column which is labelled, 'no evidence on which to make a judgement' to avoid artificially forcing an opinion out of your respondents.

Some of the statements in Table 6.5 should attract positive responses and some negatives ones. The scoring of 12345 has been reversed (54321) to accommodate this. I find this reversing of questions, some positive and some negative, helps to avoid the respondents just ticking quickly down the list of questions. The reversals make them stop and think about each question before answering it.

There are other ways of laying out such an attitude survey, depending upon the information that is of interest. A fairly common format requests estimates of frequency, with dimensions like:

1 Often	1 Almost always
2 Fairly often	2 Often
3 Occasionally	3 Occasionally
4 Once in a while	4 Seldom
5 Very seldom	5 Almost never

Another requests opinions on relative importance with dimensions like:

1 Unimportant	1 Yes, to a great extent
2 Of little importance	2 Yes, to some extent
3 Rather important	3 Neither yes nor no
4 Very important	4 No, not particularly
5 Absolutely essential	5 No, definitely not

Describing survey results

With all of these formats, a set of frequencies will be calculated to represent the opinions given. These may be published as raw figures if the numbers are small, but it is better to convert them to percentages where the numbers are large. Whether a number is 'large' is to some extent a matter of judgement. Reporting results is intended to inform people, and the audience must be considered. My view would be that for numbers less than 50, the raw frequencies will give more information. For numbers above 50 it becomes less likely that the raw figures will be easily understood.

For instance, in the example below, the actual numbers are useful because changes in individual perceptions during the programme would be of interest:

The evaluation of training is:								
A carefully planned process with a set agenda	1	0	4	6	2	0	1	Changing throughout as the focus changes during the process

On the other hand, in an organisation-wide survey, the clarity may be enhanced by conversion of the raw figures to percentages, as these are easier to understand. For example, in a survey on subordinates' views of their managers' styles, the following raw figures were obtained from 194 respondents:

Your supervisor:	**A**	**TA**	**U**	**TD**	**D**
Delegates sufficient authority and responsibility to you	54	81	31	14	14

I think that these figures are easier to understand and discuss when expressed as percentages; indeed, many people will start converting them roughly in their heads or on pieces of paper to improve their understanding. In this case the conversion is fairly simple as the population is close to 200:

Your supervisor:	A	TA	U	TD	D
Delegates sufficient authority and responsibility to you	28	42	16	7	7

It is, of course, important to make some statement in the table of results of the survey about just what the size of the population of respondents was. In this case the statement would be, 'Percentages based 194 responses to the 203 questionnaires distributed'. It is also important that the respondents are representative of the part of the organisation being surveyed. This may mean either a high proportion or a very carefully selected sample.

IN BRIEF

Attitudes are not as easy to measure as levels of knowledge or skills. They may, however, be equally important in predicting performance levels. It may thus be worthwhile assessing attitudes even when the main aim is an increase in knowledge or skills.

Self-efficacy – the perception that a particular situation or task can be handled successfully – seems to be a particularly good predictor of future performance. This is probably because it is associated with willingness to try something, and persistence in the face of difficulty. Training events should be designed to develop this attitude and could be evaluated in terms of how successful they have been in so doing.

Attitude surveys are one way of assessing the 'internal processes' aspects of organisational effectiveness. These measures can be affected by events that have nothing to do with training. However, it is possible to include in such surveys specific questions that can measure changes in attitudes that are likely to be affected by management behaviour, and thus collect evidence on the effectiveness of management development activities.

There is an extensive literature on measuring attitudes, and it has not been possible to discuss it in any depth within this book. Interested readers who would like further information on employee surveys might like to read Walters (1996). Those who are more interested in measuring individual attitudes should find Henerson, Morris et al (1978) useful.

REFERENCES AND FURTHER READING

BANDURA A. (1986) *Social Foundations of Thought and Action*. Englewood Cliffs, N.J., Prentice-Hall.

DONNISON P.A. (1993) *The Effect of Outdoor Management Development on Self-efficacy*. Unpublished MSc dissertation. Birkbeck College, University of London.

HENERSON M.E., MORRIS L.L. *and* FITZGIBBON C.T. (1978) *How to Measure Attitudes*. Beverley Hills, Sage.

STAJKOVIC A.D. *and* LUTHANS F. (1998) 'Self-efficacy and work-related performance: A meta-analysis'. *Psychological Bulletin. 124,* 2, 240–261.

THAYER P.W. *and* TEACHOUT M.S. (1995) *A climate for transfer model*. Rep. No. AL/HR-TP-1995-0035, Brooks Air Force Base.

WALTERS M. (1996) *Employee Attitude and Opinion Surveys*. London, IPD.

7 ■ EVALUATION BEFORE DESIGNING A LEARNING EVENT

Evaluating *before* the event may sound like an odd idea to those who are more familiar with evaluation as the end of the training cycle. However, very few training events are planned, designed and run if it is not thought likely that they will result in some learning that will be of benefit to the organisation. Someone, usually the training manager, has carried out an evaluation, in the sense of judging the likely value of the activity, as part of the decision to run the programme. If this evaluation is to be more than just an opinion, some analysis will need to be made of the likely benefit and the likely cost of the activities. A number of ways in which this pre-evaluation can be done will be discussed in this chapter.

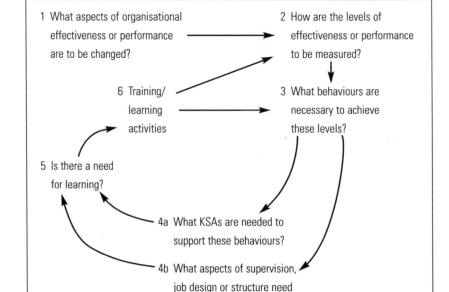

Stage 5 in the model is a pre-evaluation of how likely it is that a training activity will be the best way of facilitating the changes that are necessary. The trend is towards smaller training departments and, if these are to have a significant impact on organisational effectiveness, the training that they provide must be that which adds value.

THE MANAGEMENT OF PERFORMANCE

The pre-evaluation will also incorporate stage 4b in the model, as it will be important to examine the context in which performance is expected. The level of performance shown by people in the workplace cannot be predicted from their ability alone, because it is not just a function of knowledge and skills. Attitudes are important and so are opportunities and priorities. A better way to predict performance is to look at three aspects:

Performance = Ability × Motivation × Opportunity.

The multiplication signs mean that if there is no ability, or no motivation, or no opportunity, there will be a zero level of performance. Some amount of each of these three factors needs to be present.

The decision to use training to improve performance usually implies that ability needs to be increased. However, as we saw above, the level of motivation can also be increased by learning. People who are confident that they can do some task (those who have high self-efficacy) are more likely to attempt it than those whose confidence is low. They are also more likely to persist in trying to do it if it does not go well the first time.

Motivation can be increased in the work context without carrying out any training for the job-holders. Managers can improve performance by setting agreed targets, monitoring progress, assisting when things are not going well, encouragement and praise when things go well. They can also set different priorities and tasks so that the 'opportunity' part of the equation is affected. It could well be that such changes in supervisory practice could achieve the changes in the behaviour of employees, and thus the desired increases in performance, without training the job-holders. If the pre-evaluation can establish that this is the case, then the training investment might be better spent on short 'performance management' workshops for managers rather than training for the job-holders.

If the analysis reveals that it is also necessary to increase the ability of the job-holders, the intervention will often entail a mixture of changing styles of supervision, tasking, performance management, and learning to achieve the desired changes in behaviour and thus effectiveness. This is 'state-of-the-art' training, and evaluation procedures are central to it because the measurement of performance, and the identification of blocks to performance, are crucial to success. Managers and supervisors must be involved in these training and development activities because they must set the organisational context to support learning. It also helps if they are involved in the delivery.

For example, in an attempt to guarantee the longer-term survival of a company that produces computers and the software to run them it was decided that the marketing function should be radically overhauled. The intention was to produce what the customers wanted rather than try to sell what the company produced. The marketing function would, therefore, take over the leadership of the organisation from the engineers. Central to the change was a six-week programme for sales reps, and this was designed and delivered (with some outside help) by the area sales managers. These latter developed the new model, taught it, and later supervised reps using it with customers. A successful change, which rescued the company, was thus based upon institutionalising new methods for marketing products, not just by changing attitudes and skills, but also by increasing supervisory involvement to make sure that the new methods were used.

The process that is being described is one of improving performance by changing the way in which things are done at work. It is, therefore, worthwhile to consider a simple model of organisational change, in order to clarify what is required. Such a model is shown in Figure 7.1.

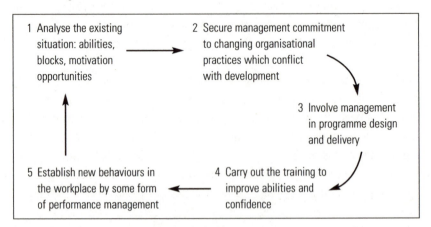

Figure 7.1: Training as organisational change

Measurement and evaluation are key aspects of phases 1 and 5 of the model. It should also be clear that facilitating the learning is not solely the responsibility of the trainers.

The managers or supervisors are also involved to the ensure the relevance of what is being learned, and continuity of the development of the learning, so that it results in changes in the ways that work activities are carried out. They have the key role of assisting transfer of the learning by monitoring performance and encouraging the new ways of doing the work.

CLIMATE FOR TRANSFER

Exactly what supervisors and managers ought to be doing in order to facilitate transfer was, until recently, not very clear. A landmark study (Rouiller and Goldstein 1993), which introduced the concept of 'climate for transfer' into the literature on training, helps to clarify this.

The study describes the evaluation of a nine-week training course for assistant managers in a fast-food chain (with some 100 outlets). The expected behaviour of the assistant managers when they were at work was described in a list of 92 behaviours (things like: checks deliveries, makes sure that the product is in good condition, makes sure that the oldest product is used first). These 92 behaviours shaped the content of the course and the knowledge of the procedures involved was measured before, during and after the programme.

At the end of the programme, the 102 trained assistant managers were posted to a large number of restaurants. Each of these restaurants was assessed on a set of scales for measuring the 'Climate for Transfer'. These scales were groups of questions about:

- the extent to which goals were set and by whom

- how like the behaviour scale the normal behaviour of managers in the restaurant actually was

- the availability of equipment etc used on the programme

- the extent to which the assistant managers were allowed to handle problems

- whether positive feedback was given for the use of learned behaviour

- whether negative feedback was given for not doing the things that they were supposed to do

- whether the use of learned behaviours was punished by ridicule

- whether no feedback was given because other managers were too busy to notice what the new person was doing.

Some weeks after the programme, the work of the assistant managers was monitored against a checklist of the 92 expected behaviours. How many of the behaviours were being used and whether they were being used appropriately was converted into a 'transfer score' for each assistant manager. The important finding for us is that the amount learned during training predicted only 8 per cent of this score. The 'climate for transfer' measure of the particular restaurant in which the assistant manager was working, predicted 46 per cent.

This implies that, in this particular situation, the 'motivation' and 'opportunity' aspects of our performance equation were much more powerful than the 'ability' aspect, even though this was a nine-week course. If the learning is to be valuable, the line managers and other colleagues need to be encouraging the use of it. What they should be doing is clearly described in the list of questions above.

In terms of evaluating before designing a learning event, an important aspect of analysing the organisational context (as suggested by stage 4b in Figure 1.2, page 6) will be to assess the climate that might or might not support any learning. A follow-up study (Tracey, Tannenbaum et al 1995) on transfer climate emphasises just how important this is.

This second study describes the evaluation of a three-day, off-job workshop for departmental managers in a supermarket chain (77 stores). In each store there was one manager, one assistant manager and some 10 departmental managers. These latter were taken out in groups over a five-month period for three-day workshops to learn the interpersonal skills essential to 'customer and employee relations'. Once again, learning was assessed before and after the workshop for each of the 104 departmental managers involved. Behaviour was also assessed before and after, this time on a set of 18 items (1–5 frequency scores on each item), to discover how frequently they were doing the things expected of someone who was good at 'customer and employee relationships'.

The 'before and after' measures of learning showed that quite a lot was achieved during the programme but, in this study, the amount of post-training knowledge did not predict the on-job behaviour, ie the learning did not transfer. The best predictor of post-training behaviour was pre-training behaviour; what they did afterwards was very like what they did before the workshop. The study also confirmed that the transfer climate measure was a useful predictor of behaviour; the activities of the manager and the assistant manager greatly affected the post-training behaviour of the departmental managers who had undergone the training.

What all of this means is that, in this case, the three-day workshop had no effect on the desired behaviours (which were thought to show better customer and employee relationships). The investment would have been better aimed at changing the behaviour of the manager and the assistant manager and then requiring them to 'cascade' the new behaviours that were desired by the company. Without their positive involvement, no changes were possible. This is an important and unusual study because of the careful research involved, but I am sure that it reflects the experience of many of us. Short workshops which try to change the behaviour of people will usually fail if the organisational culture does not encourage the changes being proposed.

Cost-effectiveness comparisons

Sometimes more than one training approach could be considered. For instance, should we buy in someone to run a particular activity or should we run it with our own people? One of the criteria on which the alternatives should be compared is the cost of providing the training. The costs of each approach would be estimated and the alternatives compared on this basis.

It is usually assumed, by accountants, that the expected outcomes are the same and thus that one should simply select the cheaper alternative. This may account for the quantity of training that is now 'outsourced' to training consultancies. There are, however, added benefits from providing training internally. For instance:

■ The training needs analysis might be done more thoroughly by an internal trainer than by a line manager who buys someone in to deal with his problem.

■ The internal training department should be better aware of organisational priorities and plans and should, therefore, see more ways of integrating the training with work tasks.

■ The mix between what the supervisors will do and what the trainers will do might be easier to agree when the trainer has regular contact with that department on a range of training issues.

■ The follow-up evaluation and continuity of learning into the work will probably require an internal trainer anyway.

I do not want to be unduly critical of the principle of buying-in training. There are many training providers who work on a regular basis with an organisation and can offer most of the advantages of internal trainers, plus some greater flexibility and experience, at a lower cost. Some, however, are selling standard packages and claiming that these can be tailored during the event to suit the delegates' objectives. The perceptive reader of this book will not be surprised to learn that I am suspicious of this. My view is that a careful analysis should be made of the behaviours that need changing, in order to improve effectiveness, *before the training is designed*.

A simple example might help to clarify some of the issues involved in cost-effectiveness comparisons.

Suppose that the cost of a full-time trainer is £25,000 salary plus £10,000 a year for overheads. Such a person could deliver some 35 five-day courses/workshops a year and still have time for needs identification, preparation and holiday. The cost of delivery of a five-day programme for (say) 10 participants with two trainers would thus be £2,000 plus the overheads of cost of training rooms etc.

Training consultants will provide training at rates that vary between £500 for one trainer and £2,000 for more than one trainer per day. Taking a rate of £1,000 for two trainers, the cost of the five-day programme would be £5,000 (again plus rooms etc).

The cost of sending 10 participants on an open course run by an agency might be some £500 per day per delegate, ie £25,000.

The costs can be easily compared, but there are other questions about effectiveness, which might include the following:

- Can sufficient participants be provided to justify two trainers for 35 weeks?

- Can the trainers cover enough topics to offer 35 really useful weeks per year?

- How does 14 weeks (two-fifths of 35) with different consultants compare with 35 weeks with two internal trainers (range of topics, expertise, number of delegates)?

- If external consultants are to provide the training, who will do the needs analysis with the line manager?

- Which method of delivery is likely to provide the most *effective* training, given the problems of the organisational context and transfer of the learning.

Where two methods of delivery are to be considered, it is possible to estimate the costs and compare the likely effectiveness of the two programmes and then offer a rationale for deciding whether the increased effectiveness of one programme justifies the extra cost. This comparison is more convincing when pilot versions of the two programmes can be run, so that actual, rather than estimated, levels of effectiveness can be used.

For example, one of the High Street clearing banks was interested to compare the use of computer-based learning (CBL) with delivering a traditional five-day off-job programme. The course was designed to teach some aspects of bank work connected with lending money on mortgages. It was a knowledge-based programme, and some of it was at the 'analytical' level, ie analysing a situation so that the correct procedure can be selected (p.54). The CBL package was produced and, in piloting, it was found that the average trainee could complete it in three days. It was intended that the three days would be spent in the branch at which the trainee worked, or one very near it, and that the learning should be spaced at regular intervals during slack periods.

Costings were made for the development, delivery and evaluation of the CBL method. The delivery aspect was rather provisional as it was not known just how much co-ordination would be necessary for it to work well. (One of the problems with open learning systems is to achieve the amount of structure that is necessary to allow the trainees to develop their learning in a systematic way. An hour or so here and there does not produce optimum learning.) The traditional five-day course had been running for some time and could be costed accurately. The development costs were spread over the number of people likely to be trained in three years. It was thus possible to make a comparison on the basis of estimated cost per student trained on each of the systems.

The systems could also be compared on an estimate of effectiveness:

■ shorter training time and less time away from work for the CBL system

■ less travel time and expense for the CBL package

■ less covering costs for trainees on the CBL package

■ better learning gain on the CBL package

■ some increment in computer literacy among staff using CBL.

A further basis for comparison of effectiveness would be the preference of the trainees for the methods being offered. Some would, no doubt, like to get away from the workplace for five days. Some would like to learn with others. There may also be some benefit in their discussing how the work is organised in different branches.

COST/BENEFIT ANALYSIS

Another aspect of pre-evaluation is that of establishing whether the likely benefits are worth the cost involved in achieving them. Here we are not just asking the question, 'Are there cheaper ways of doing this?' We also need to ask, 'Is it worthwhile doing this at all? What will it cost? What is the likely return?

Before the learning events are designed, an attempt is made to identify the likely changes in behaviour of those who are to undergo the training. A group of interested parties, usually some of the supervisors/managers and some of the trainers, discuss what is intended in terms of changes in effectiveness and the behaviours needed to achieve these. It is often valuable to include the views of other stakeholders (for instance, some of those to be trained and some 'customers' who receive services or products from them) in these discussions. The results of such discussion can be summarised in a simple table like that shown in Table 7.1.

Table 7.1: A list of behaviours expected after training

After training the delegates are likely to have different levels of skill and of motivation, for example:			
Improved skills	New skills	More likely to	Less likely to
1...............	1...............	1...............	1...............
2...............	2...............	2...............	2...............
3...............	3...............	3...............	3...............
Etc...............			

When the desired changes in behaviour have been identified, each of the stakeholders is asked to list the benefits likely to result from these, seen from his or her perspective. A possible prompt list is shown in Table 7.2.

Table 7.2 is a simple checklist to aid the discussion of what benefits might be realised through the proposed training activity. It should, however, be clear to those who started at the beginning of this book that we are talking here about a process that was described earlier under the heading of 'Impact Analysis' on pp. 13 to 15. Further lists of possible benefits are to be found in Chapter 2, which has as its main aim the description and measurement of aspects of organisational effectiveness. Most of these aspects can be used to develop the 'benefits' side of the equation. The 'cost' side will be discussed more fully later in this chapter.

Sometimes the expected benefits can be directly converted to a cash value, but this is not the main purpose of cost/benefit analysis. The intention is to provide a rational basis for making the decision – to train or not to train.

An alternative approach to analysing the benefits from investment in training was developed in the IPD report, *What makes Training Pay?* (Lee 1996). Two forms of benefit are described, 'pay-back' and 'pay-forward'. Pay-back means a return on investment that is measurable in financial or analogous terms, ie increases in some form of effectiveness – individual, team or part of the organisation – which can be seen as a direct return on investment in training. Pay-forward describes a benefit from investment in training that cannot be expressed directly in financial terms. Usually this implies changes in behaviour, such as increased flexibility or ability to learn and change.

For isolated, remedial or tactical training interventions, pay-back is usually the focus as the objective will be to improve effectiveness in some specific part of the

▶ Table 7.2: A checklist of possible benefits

List of possible benefits to:

Trainees

improved job prospects

higher earnings

access to more interesting jobs

improved job satisfaction etc.

Supervisors/line managers

increased output

higher value of output

better quality, less waste

more flexible, innovative

likely to stay longer

less likely to be sick/stressed

less likely to be absent

less need to be supervised

increased safety

decrease in accidents etc.

Customers

better quality work or service

less need to return work

more 'on time' deliveries

more customised service etc.

organisation. If base-line measures are taken before the intervention is made, this increase in effectiveness will usually have a measurable benefit.

Where the training and development strategy is intended to support the longer-term objectives of the organisation, pay-forward measures become more important. Changes in behaviour will be assessed by using attitude surveys and behaviour scales, and the intention is to discover if these are in a direction consistent with that thought appropriate for implementing longer-term organisation strategy.

It is, of course, likely that both forms of benefit will be observed from some types of developmental activity. One of the case studies in the IPD report (Lee 1996) describes a programme developed in ICL to facilitate 'beneficial change'. Senior technical staff attended a programme intended to focus their attention on the need for continuous change and innovation as being central to the survival of the company. Each delegate then attempted to implement a change project in his or her area of responsibility. They could count on the support of their managers and colleagues and also had the assistance of a change agent. Reports on the projects were produced and circulated to all of the delegates as a way of maintaining the impetus started by the course. Some of the projects produced significant financial benefits to the company (pay-back which could be used to justify the cost of the programme). Of perhaps greater significance was that most of the delegates from the early programmes, when they had completed their set projects, embarked on fresh projects on their own initiative; a significant pay-forward benefit of improving the company's ability to innovate and initiate change.

Cost/benefit can be an involved process, and a full discussion of it is beyond the scope of this book. For readers who are interested in further detail and a range of worked examples, I would suggest the books by Phillips published by the American Society for Training and Development (Phillips 1994; 1997).

COSTING

A book on evaluating changes would not be complete without some mention of costing. Although few trainers carry out detailed costing activities, some flavour of what is involved is useful in thinking through the logic of evaluation. Costing methods and systems will vary, and liaison with the finance department will ensure that the procedure adopted for establishing training costs is compatible with those used in other parts of the organisation. A simple framework for estimating costs that I have found useful is given below.

	Personnel	Facilities	Equipment
Design	1a	1b	1c
Delivery	2a	2b	2c
Evaluation	3a	3b	3c

Design

The cost of design can be spread over the life of the programme (ie shared by the proposed number of programmes) as it will otherwise account for some 50 per cent of the overall costs. As a rough guideline, technical courses will need some five hours of preparation per hour of delivery. Programmed or packaged instruction will be much more expensive, as up to 100 hours of design are needed for one hour of instruction. With computer-based learning the ratio can be as high as 400:1.

The cost of *designing* the learning event might include things like:

1a Costs of preliminary analysis of training needs, development of objectives, course development, lesson planning, programming, audio-visual aids production, consultant advice, contractors

1b Offices, telephones

1c Production of workbooks, slides, tapes, tests, programmes, printing and reproduction.

Delivery

The cost of actually running the event might include:

2a Some proportion of annual salaries of trainers, lecturers, trainees, clerical/-administrative staff. Costs of consultants and outside lecturers. Travel costs

2b Cost of conference centres or up-keep of classrooms, buildings, offices; accommodation and food; office supplies and expenses

2c Equipment for delivering the training – slide projectors, videos, computers, simulators, workbooks, maintenance and repair of aids; expendable training materials or some proportion of cost relative to lifetime; handouts; hire of films, videos etc.

Evaluation

The cost of evaluation is usually low compared to the other two elements. Possible costs include:

3a Cost of designing questionnaires etc, follow-up interviews, follow-up focus groups, travel, accommodation; analysis and summary of data collected; delivering the evaluation report

3b Offices, telephones

3c Tests, questionnaires, postage.

To give a complete picture, it is also worth considering a general overhead for the expense of maintaining the training department. This may be allocated to individual training programmes on the basis of hours of participant learning, tutor involvement and level of administration required.

Salaries of trainees are often not allocated to training costs on the basis that a certain amount of 'slack' is necessary for effectiveness. For instance, when a foreman is taken off the factory floor for a few hours a week to discuss supervisory methods, it makes very little difference to his 'output' as a foreman. In such a case it seems hardly worthwhile to include the value of his salary for the hours spent as a cost to training. However, most surveys report that the salary of trainees averages about a third of all training costs. If this is estimated to be a reasonable figure for a programme that is being planned, then it would seem worthwhile to include these costs. Similarly, I would argue that any 'covering costs' incurred because of trainees' absence from the workplace should be included.

Having established the cost of a training programme and the value of the benefits, a return on investment (ROI) can be calculated from the formula:

$$ROI = \frac{\text{Value of Benefits} - \text{Training Costs}}{\text{Training Costs}} \times 100\%$$

For example, one of the case studies reported in the 2001 National Training Awards describes an improvement in efficiency in cleaning services at a university and estimates the value of the benefit as £135k. This benefit resulted from increases in efficiency in the deployment of staff and decreases in the very high absenteeism and staff turnover rates. The training cost was estimated as £21k for training supervisors and persuading them to cascade the new methods down the organisation.

$$ROI = \frac{135 - 21}{21} \times 100 = \frac{114}{21} \times 100 = 543\%$$

Decision criteria on what might be an acceptable return vary, but most organisations will accept a positive return of 10 or 20 per cent, particularly if there are also other desirable (but unmeasurable) benefits. This leads us to one of the 'yes, buts' about ROI calculations: they capture only the 'pay-back' value of the benefits of the training. In this case of cleaning services, a change in morale and self-esteem is reported, as well as a greater openness to adopting new and more efficient working methods. As we have seen, this sort of 'pay-forward' benefit is often more valuable to the organisation than the short-term gain that can be converted to a financial benefit.

A second 'yes, but' is that the simple statistic produced from an ROI calculation often obscures many of the other things that have happened. The NTA report (2001) includes descriptions of changes in management structures, using the supervisors to cascade new ideas, changes in methods of performance management, the setting of new standards, and the production of a manual of procedures. None of these changes to the organisational context appear on the cost side of the equation, but they could have profound effects on the efficiency of the workforce.

MATCHING METHODS TO OUTCOMES

As well as thinking about the mix between training and changes in the organisational context, it is worthwhile considering whether the proposed *methods* are likely to achieve the desired outcomes.

At a basic level this might mean simply that, if you want a skilled performance, the people need more than just the knowledge of how to do it. They will also need to do it a number of times and to practise to improve the level of performance. At a more general level, the evidence is that the approach taken in training should resemble the expected performance (Kraiger (ed) 2002).

If you want people to be able to solve particular types of problem, say when 'troubleshooting' on a piece of electronic equipment, the best strategy for teaching them to classify and approach problems will be one that teaches them how to think – a cognitive approach. Ideas on how experts would approach the problem, what they would look for, what sub-goals they would set, how they would decide whether they were making progress, are the types of learning that would be needed. Essentially, the process is one of building up a 'mental map' of the area of interest.

If you want supervisors to be able to motivate their subordinates, teaching them theories of motivation will not be sufficient. Theories may be useful to provide frameworks to help the learners make sense of their experience; knowledge of theory is, however, usually not sufficient to change the way in which people interact with others. A behavioural approach, which encourages them to bring in actual problems, discuss them with other supervisors, role-play them and try out various ways of dealing with the situation, is much more likely to succeed than a theory-based programme (Goldstein and Sorcher 1974; Latham and Saari 1979). The key aspect is that they actually try ways of doing it, use their experience, and then talk about what happened and why. They do not just listen to someone telling them how.

One way to think about this is to try to design learning activities which take the learners all the way around the Kolb cycle (Kolb 1984). A version of this is shown in Figure 7.2.

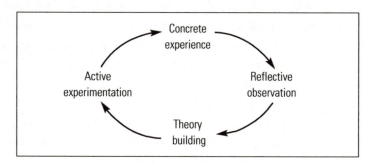

Figure 7.2: The Kolb cycle of learning

In order to learn effectively, the trainees will need to have some experience. Learning should start from where they are and it needs to be related to their experience, if it is to make sense in an organisational context. If they have no experience in the particular area of interest, the training will have to provide it.

As a second stage, they need some framework in which to make sense of the experience. They need to stop and reflect about what the experience means, which aspects of it are important, and so on. Usually they will need to share this reflective stage with others, and it often helps for a trainer to facilitate this.

The third stage is one of 'theory building'. This simply means that they change the way in which they think about events like those that they have experienced. In many cases, this will entail thinking about ways which might be successful in handling particular situations.

The fourth stage is that of actively trying some of these ways to see if they will actually be successful. This completes the cycle because it implies further concrete (actual) experience.

It is likely that adults need to go around this cycle a couple of times before they change the way in which they do things. The most successful way to build up self-efficacy is to help the learner to achieve some mastery of the situation by going around a learning cycle like that above (Latham and Saari 1979). It may be possible for a schoolteacher to convince young children that they can do something by some form of encouragement, but with older children, and certainly with adults, it is usually necessary for them to try it for themselves and thus become convinced that they can do it.

What I am suggesting here is that an important part of the pre-evaluation of a learning activity that is intended to change work behaviours should be to examine whether it will take the trainees all the way around the cycle. If not, some thought must be given to who will be responsible for 'active experimentation' and consolidation of learning.

It is interesting in this context to examine the enthusiasm for modern forms of computer based-learning (intranet, extranet, e-learning). Both American (Bassi and van Buren 1999) and British (CIPD 2003) surveys have shown a significant increase in the use of such media, and great claims are being made for them (for instance, IRS 2002). However, as an evaluator, one should advise a little cautious analysis before being swept away by the enthusiasm.

- Such media offer greater flexibility, as the trainees can learn when they want to. However, learning that is not monitored by checking progress and sorting out problems is often inefficient, and many organisations have found it difficult to set up an effective infrastructure for doing this (Brown and Ford 2002).

- There is some evidence that these methods reduce the time taken to learn the material, but this is usually due to the level of analysis of the subject matter before it is assembled into a learning package (Brown and Ford 2002).

- Poorly designed training, or that which is not specifically tailored to the target population and the company culture, will not initiate useful learning regardless of the extent to which appealing or expensive technology is used to deliver it (Brown and Ford 2002).

- Although the cost of developing such material is very high, reduced costs of employing trainers, travel costs and covering costs for trainees should, in time, cover this. It is interesting to note that few studies have actually shown cost savings (Whalen and Wright 2000) as system maintenance, technical support and upgrading of content, software and hardware are expensive.

The methods are potentially very efficient for delivering learning at levels 1 and 2 in our hierarchies (basic information and procedures). Provided the audience is large enough and the material is relatively long-lived, they could also be cost-effective. It is, however, clear that the success of training in changing work-based behaviour is determined not only by the quality of the training, but by many aspects of the organisational context.

Those of us who have been in training a long time may be permitted a wry smile when faced with the present enthusiasm for e-learning. In the 1960s and early 1970s, very similar claims were being made for 'programmed learning'(PL). This largely failed to realise its potential because:

- The designers were a long way away from the learners, both physically and in their understanding of the organisational context.

- Needs were not properly identified, as too broad a view was taken about the target population. There was a tendency to buy something produced somewhere else which 'should be appropriate for our people'.

- No one accepted responsibility for monitoring the progress of the learners; they were expected to know what they wanted, and how, and when to get it.

- There was little attempt to integrate the learning with work experience.

- The pace of change in the nature of people's work, and the skills to do it well, made it uneconomic. Development costs were not recovered by spreading use of the packages over years.

In the 1970s and 1980s similar claims were being made for computer-based learning, and enthusiasts set up departments in large organisations dedicated to the production of CBL packages. Sadly, to a large extent these failed for the reasons listed above. Talking to people in such departments was depressing because few of them knew anything about the PL literature and most thought it irrelevant. Now the fashion has turned to e-learning and, from what they are writing, the enthusiasts seem likely to make the same mistakes again.

Many of the factors associated with the effectiveness of training are independent of the media used, and training designers ignore them at their peril. We shall return to this discussion in the next chapter in the section on evaluating the training process.

CHANGING ATTITUDES

Changing attitudes is more difficult than changing levels of knowledge or skills. If we are to achieve the higher levels on our continuum (p. 79) of 'preference for the new methods' and 'incorporation into normal routines', those who are learning will have to change the ways in which they think and discover advantages in the new ways. This means taking them around this cycle of learning (Figure 7.2) more than once – doing it, thinking about it, trying it in different ways until satisfied with the new ways and willing to discard the old.

For instance, it has proved to be difficult to teach car drivers to wear seat belts by giving them information. Even when they realise that many injuries can be avoided by wearing a seat belt, this is not sufficient. It has been found to be necessary to *make* drivers wear them by making it a statutory requirement. One of the effects of this has been that fastening the belt has become incorporated into normal routines for driving. Most people now feel uncomfortable when they have *not* fastened the belt. Their attitudes have changed after they have had to change their behaviour. I am sure that there are many other examples of this in the 'equal opportunities' field, where early approaches were based upon giving information and hoping that this would result in changes in behaviour. These approaches have (largely) been replaced by statements of what kind of behaviour is expected and the introduction of sanctions for infringing these codes.

IN BRIEF

If the intention is to improve performance by changing behaviour, some evaluation should be carried out *before* a learning activity is designed and run, to decide:

- whether learning is necessary or whether some form of performance management will achieve the desired changes

- how the learning will be integrated with other changes in the organisational context (for instance: goal-setting, priorities, job-design and tasking, structure, climate for innovation)

- what level of involvement of supervisors and colleagues will be necessary to support the new ways of carrying out the work.

A further question that should be asked before running training activities is whether the cost is justified by the probable benefits.

- When it is thought necessary to carry out the activities, this question may be answered by considering a number of ways of providing the learning opportunities and selecting the one that seems to offer best value for money.

- When there is some doubt about the need, a listing of the possible benefits will give some basis for making the decision.

- Where safety or accident rates are concerned, the question may be a rather different one, 'Can we afford *not* to run the training?' This question might also be posed for events that are intended to increase the flexibility of staff or their ability to innovate.

Evaluation before an event might also focus on the proposed methods and ask whether they are likely to be effective in achieving change. Knowledge and theory may be necessary but, if behavioural change is expected, some practice of the type of behaviour that is expected will be required. A sound, general principle of training design is that methods should be matched to outcomes. Some of the expected outcomes are actually forms of organisational change and, where this is the case, aspects of the organisational context will need to be considered. For instance, it may be necessary to change the reward system (by encouragement and sanctions) as well as attitudes and levels of knowledge. It may also be necessary to establish a positive climate for transfer.

This pre-activity evaluation, of the likelihood that a proposed training activity will result in the increased performance desired, is a key aspect of evaluation as 'control'. In my experience, it is not often carried out with any degree of sophistication. This is usually because the links between those responsible for training and line managers are not close enough to make it possible.

What is happening in your organisation?

Have you put procedures in place to ensure that most of the investment in training will result in improved performance?

REFERENCES AND FURTHER READING

BASSI L.J. *and* VAN BUREN M.E. (1999) *The 1999 ASTD State of the Industry Report.* Washington DC, American Society for Training and Development.

BROWN K.G. *and* FORD J.K. (2002) 'Using computer technology in training: Building an infrastructure for active learning'. In Kraiger (ed) *Creating, implementing and maintaining effective training and development: State-of-the-art lessons for practice.* San Francisco, Jossey-Bass.

CIPD (2003) *Training and Development 2003.* London, CIPD.

GOLDSTEIN G.A.P. *and* SORCHER M. (1974) *Changing Supervisor Behavior.* New York, Pergammon Press.

KRAIGER K. (ed) (2002) *Creating, Implementing and Managing Effective Training and Development: State of the Art lessons in Practice.* San Francisco: Jossey-Bass. (Particularly Chapter 3 by Noe and Colquitt, Chapter 7 by Brown and Ford, and Chapter 9 by Machin)

IRS (2002) Delivering an e-learning package. 'Employment Trends'. *IRS Employment Review. 753.*

KOLB D.A. (1984) *Experiential Learning.* Englewood Cliffs, NY, Prentice-Hall.

LATHAM G.P. *and* SAARI L.M. (1979) 'The Application of social learning theory to training supervisors through behavioural modelling'. *Journal of Applied Psychology. 64,* 239–246.

LEE R. (1996) *What Makes Training Pay?* London, IPD.

NATIONAL TRAINING AWARDS (2001) University of Sheffield (Facilities Management Directorate).

PHILLIPS J.J. (ed) (1994) *Measuring Return on Investment Volume 1.* ASTD.

PHILLIPS J.J. (ed) (1997) *Measuring Return on Investment Volume 2.* ASTD.

ROUILLER J.Z. *and* GOLDSTEIN I.L. (1993) 'Transfer Climate and Positive Transfer'. *Human Resource Development Quarterly 4.* 4, 337–390.

TRACEY B.J., TANNENBAUM S.I. *and* KAVANAGH M.J. (1995) 'Applying Trained Skills on the Job: The Importance of the Work Environment'. *Journal of Applied Psychology 80.* 2, 239–252.

WHALEN T. *and* WRIGHT D. (2000) *The business case for web-based training.* Norwood Mass, Artech House.

8 ■ EVALUATION DURING THE EVENT

Stage 6 of our model of training is an acknowledgement that learning activities are required to facilitate changes in behaviour and effectiveness. If these activities are to be carried out efficiently and effectively, evaluation should be used during the learning to ensure that it meets the objectives set for it by the various interested parties. Evaluation can also be used to 'benchmark' the design and delivery of the activities against best practice.

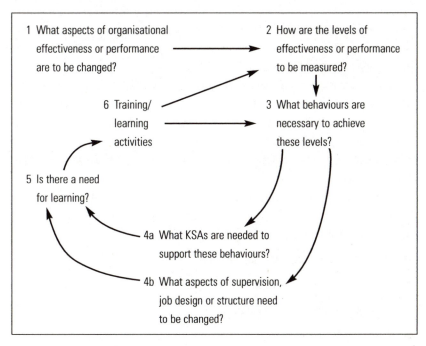

1 What aspects of organisational effectiveness or performance are to be changed?

2 How are the levels of effectiveness or performance to be measured?

6 Training/ learning activities

3 What behaviours are necessary to achieve these levels?

5 Is there a need for learning?

4a What KSAs are needed to support these behaviours?

4b What aspects of supervision, job design or structure need to be changed?

▌ ESTABLISHING THE OBJECTIVES

The clarification of the objectives, the reasons for learning, and the expectations of the three main interested parties (usually the trainees, their managers and the organisation) are important as a basis for later evaluation. The processes involved in this are, of course, also necessary for the design of the activities and their integration into organisational priorities. The objectives that are of most value are those that are quite specific about what kinds of behaviour change are expected, ie what employees will be able to do that they could not do before, what they will do more of, and what they will do less of. Such objectives set goals and targets for the learning and are thus motivating for the learners, providing they accept some ownership for the targets (Locke and Latham 1990).

One aspect of evaluating is therefore to establish that the trainees have objectives, that these are in line with those of other interested parties and that the trainees are, to some extent, committed to achieving them. A well-organised training system will usually ensure that this is done *before* the programme of learning begins. The line manager, together with a trainer, will establish exactly what the training need is. The trainee will be involved in this, at least to the extent of discussing with the line manager what the objectives are and what changes are expected. Desirable though such a practice is, the CIPD 2003 survey reported that only 22 per cent of organisations surveyed said that 'all' received a pre-training briefing, and a further 30 per cent that 'a majority' received such a briefing (CIPD 2003).

When the programme is a long one, it may also be worthwhile for the trainer/tutor to talk at some length with the trainee about aims and objectives, possible content and likely style of delivery. Where this does not happen, the early part of the programme itself will need to be used to establish what the objectives are and create some desire to learn what is necessary to achieve them. There are numbers of ways in which this might be done.

For instance, with off-the-job programmes of more than two days it may be possible to interview each of the participants in the evenings and talk these things over in a fairly informal way. Questions that might be useful for this are:

- How did you hear about the programme?

- Why did you want to come on it?

- What are you hoping to get out of it?

- How will this help you in your work?

- How is it going so far?

- Are the methods being used helping you to learn?

■ Is there anything we should be doing differently?

One purpose is to try to assess how close the programme is to what the trainees expected (that is, how good the pre-course information and briefing was). Another is to try to discover variations in the objectives of the participants which might mean some redesign of the remaining parts of the programme. A third is to try to discover if the methods, pace and level of difficulty are suitable for the participants.

It is also possible to distribute copies of the aims and objectives that were set for the trainers who designed the programme, and discuss these with the participants. This tends to be a rather one-way process, of the trainers telling the trainees what is in store. It is sometimes possible to involve the participants by asking them to describe what they will do differently when they go back if they can achieve these objectives. The value in this is that it might encourage the trainees to take more 'ownership' of the objectives, and thus the learning.

Some tutors ask the participants to write up their objectives for the week on flip-chart paper and decorate the walls with these. This process does create a sense of ownership and allows the group to discover possible objectives other than those which they have recorded. It is also possible to review progress against these objectives at the end of the workshop. A possible danger in using this process is that the objectives set by the participants may have little to do with effectiveness in the workplace. For instance, I have often seen a display of objectives for an interpersonal skills workshop which looked to me like requests for personal therapy. I would prefer a process that provided a stronger link with changed behaviour and effectiveness in the workplace.

Discussion of progress

An extension of establishing the objectives to motivate the participants to learn is to hold reviews of progress. Reviewing progress and giving feedback has a motivational aspect in that it clarifies, for the learner, the gap between present and desired performance. It is usually necessary to be aware of these gaps, and be willing to do something about them if learning is to occur. It also has the function of establishing, for the tutors, what learning has taken place and what is still needed. This information may be necessary for the (re) design of the later stages in the programme.

One way of doing this is to have regular learning reviews, when the participants write down what they have found to be particularly interesting or useful during the session. Ask them to take out a separate sheet of paper, perhaps of a different colour, and then to write down the two or three things that they have found particularly interesting. Also, ask them to write down the two or three things that they think will be most useful to them when they return to the workplace. Ask them to make a note of how they intend to use these and what they think will result from this use. The discussion afterwards can be a group one, where everyone selects something to read out, or one-to-one with tutors. The discussion gives a good feel for what is going well and for what learning they are likely to take away. It can also be used to facilitate some 'reflection' into the learning process.

The frequency of these reviews is a matter of judgement. In a programme of some weeks' duration, at the end of each week would seem to be good timing. I have found that, on a four-day workshop, each evening is a good frequency. Perhaps the most useful purpose of these reviews is to focus on the *utility* of the learning during the programme. This is again an attempt to benchmark against good practice. The process can also give a basis for later evaluation of changes. Those aspects that participants have found interesting and potentially useful can be grouped into clusters to form an action plan towards the end of the programme. This takes them further around the learning cycle to 'active experimentation'. The action plan can be used as a basis for establishing what they intend to do in the six months after the programme, and it can later be used to assess what they actually achieved.

Developing and using action plans

There is little doubt that a good deal of adult behaviour is motivated by setting goals. People have plans for what they want to do, how far they want to be promoted, how they are going to impress senior people to achieve this, where they would like to be working in five years time, and so on. There is also little doubt that setting these goals affects performance, in terms of both direction and effort (Locke and Latham 1990). The greatest value of action planning is that it taps into these sources of motivation and thus can provide a bridge for transferring learning to the work situation.

The action plans that experienced people produce are different to those made by novices. They are more specific, and the sub-goals are more clearly and logically linked to the ultimate goals. One method of evaluating during a learning activity is thus to examine the quality of the action plans that the participants are producing.

The plans should be lists of statements ranked in some way. This might be by order of priority, chronological order, or in some other logical sequence. Against each statement should be a timeframe for action. The linkages between the statements should be established and, where there is likely to be some difficulty in making one of these linkages, or achieving one of the actions, a 'force-field analysis' is carried out. This simply means thinking and then writing down:

The action:_____

Those things (or people) likely to hinder achievement of the action	Those things (or people) likely to help achieve this action
a	a
b	b
c	c
d	d

The action plan is an excellent basis for follow-up of the programme. A copy might be lodged with the tutors and used for this purpose. (It should, of course, be thoroughly discussed with the line manager on return, and this would probably be the first action listed on it.) The follow-up, some six months later, would ask questions like:

■ How much of your action plan have you been able to implement?

■ Which actions are still likely, but now need a longer timeframe?

■ Which actions have been shelved, and why?

■ What positive organisational benefits have come from your actions?

Learning logs and learning contracts can provide action plans during the training activities, and provide links between them. They can be used to check on progress and to provide the basis for a follow-up interview. In the work on the use of subordinate feedback for changing the styles used by middle managers, which was mentioned earlier (p. 43), a learning contract was drawn up by each of the managers. They were given the feedback from their subordinates and then asked if there was anything positive that they could take from it. They were then asked to make out an action plan that listed what they intended to do, how they were going to do it, and how they were going to check on progress. Each signed this as a 'learning contract' (the format is shown in Table 8.1) with the consultant, and it was made the basis for a six-month review of progress. It was also used as a basis for discussion, and further planning, after the one-year follow-up of subordinates' opinions on how the style had changed (Bramley 1994).

Reactions at the end of an activity

The most popular form of evaluation is the issue of a questionnaire during, or at the end of, the programme. The purpose is said to be that it provides feedback for the tutors so that they can improve future courses. Sometimes the ratings are also used by the training manager to monitor the quality of the programme.

▶ Table 8.1: A learning contract

Objectives set	Strategy for achieving the objectives	Criteria and means of evaluating progress
Objective 1	How you intend to do it	How you intend to measure achievement
Objective 2	"	"
Objective 3	"	"
etc		
etc		
Date:	Signed:	Signed:

If the intention is to provide feedback to improve the quality of the programme, what information is required? In the Introduction (page 7) there is a list which you might glance at to refresh your memory. The aspect which concerns us here is, 'Some detail about the effectiveness of each learning situation'. If this is to be collected, a format like that in Table 8.2 would help. Here all the topics covered during the programme are listed and a series of questions asked about each.

▶ Table 8.2: End of course questionnaire

In columns 'b' and 'c' select a number which represents your opinion using the following scales:				
Almost all of the information was new		1 2 3 4 5		Told me little I didn't know already
Presentation needs no improvement		1 2 3 4 5		Presentation needs much improvement
a. Topic	b. New information	c. Presentation	d. Time More Less Right	e. This was difficult
Topic 1	1 2 3 4 5		1 2 3 4 5	
Topic 2	1 2 3 4 5		1 2 3 4 5	
Topic 3	1 2 3 4 5		1 2 3 4 5	
etc 0				

The participants should be encouraged to make open-ended comments on the back of the form. Where someone has admitted 'difficulty', this should be followed up to discover the problem.

Specific open-ended questions can be included in the questionnaire to provide information thought to be useful. Common ones are:

- What are the three best things about this course?

- What are the three worst things about this course?

- What three changes should be made to the course?

- What aspects of the process helped you to learn?

- What aspects hindered your learning?

If it is to provide really useful information, the questionnaire should be given out at the beginning of the programme and time should be given so that it can be completed stage by stage. On programmes that last longer than a week, collecting the forms at the end of each week and reviewing them might help with the detailed planning of the next week's work.

It should be clear from this that considerable detail is necessary to provide the feedback required to review the effectiveness of each learning situation. This should be worthwhile for the first two runs of a programme, when many amendments may need to be made to the order of events and the specific activities. After the first two or so runs, most of the benefit of such feedback will have been realised. When this is the case, a more economical evaluative procedure is to focus only on new topics. Questions like those in Table 8.3 could be asked about each of these new topics.

Table 8.3. Questions about a topic

■ What is your overall reaction to the session on . . .	Very good/Good/Fair/Poor
■ Will you be able to use the material (or skill) in your job?	Frequently/Sometimes/Rarely/Unlikely
■ What did you think of the presentation of the session?	Very good/Good/Fair/Poor
■ How do you think the session could be improved?	

Most organisations carry out evaluation at the 'reaction' level (Ralphs and Stephan 1986; HMSO 1989). Trainers obviously believe that it is important to discover how participants feel about the programme they have attended. Perhaps they are making an assumption that favourable reactions imply useful learning or will predict changes in behaviour. There is not much evidence to support this. The published studies in which attempts have been made to correlate levels of reaction with amount of learning or changes in work behaviour or levels of effectiveness, have shown very poor relationships (Alliger and Janak 1989; Alliger, Tannenbaum et al 1997). In general *good* reactions do not predict learning or behaviour change any better than *poor* reactions. This is probably because the information being gathered is not suitable for that purpose. Inspection of a typical set of forms usually reveals that what is being assessed is whether the training was enjoyable and interesting, whether the accommodation was comfortable, whether the tutors were liked. This is training as a branch of entertainment, and these factors may have nothing to do with learning that would support increased effectiveness.

If the completion of these forms is to be more than an end-of-course ritual, it is important to make sure that the information can be used to provide useful feedback. General questions like:

How would you rate the course overall?	POOR	1 2 3 4 5	EXCELLENT
How would you rate the tutors?	POOR	1 2 3 4 5	EXCELLENT

do not provide information which is specific enough for this purpose.

If the intention is to provide feedback for specific tutors, some of the questions listed in Table 5.1 (p. 73) might be useful. I feel certain that rating all the tutors, or even one of them, on a five-point scale is wasting time.

Similarly, I am very dubious about attempting to discover if the objectives for the programme have been achieved, by asking:

Did the course meet your objectives?	NOT AT ALL	1 2 3 4 5	TOTALLY

If, as was suggested earlier, the objectives of the various interested parties have been made specific, then more precise ways of assessing whether they have been achieved will be available. Most of these evaluations will be made in the workplace and not at the end of training.

I do not want to give the impression that I am against the principle of using of questionnaires to collect information about courses. The practice, however, often seems to be a meaningless ritual because not enough thought has been given to the reasons for collecting the information and, therefore, the type of information that would be useful.

Evaluating the running of a programme

When a programme has been running for some time, it may be possible to improve its effectiveness by examining the whole process of it. It is more likely that this would be done by a training manager than by the trainers themselves, but a checklist of questions to ask might help to focus on good practice. The following list of questions was developed to focus on key areas when carrying out inspections of training organisations (Bramley and Hullah 1987).

Target population

- Are the 'right' people coming on the programme?
- Are they coming at the right time?
- Are they being briefed properly before they come?
- What proportion are on the programme for reasons like: a rest; her turn for training; someone else dropped out?

Objectives

- What changes are expected to result from this programme in terms of:
    - individual performance levels
    - organisational effectiveness?
- Are the objectives clear and unambiguous?
- Do the tutors know the trainees' individual learning objectives? How are they taking these into account?

Course structure

- On what learning principles is the programme structured?
- Is there a satisfactory balance between practice, reflection and theoretical input?
- Is the programme the right length? The working day?
- Does the balance of the course reflect the different degrees of importance attached to the objectives?

Methods and media

- On what basis have the methods been chosen?
- Are behavioural methods being used where behaviour change is expected?
- Are mental maps being built up where problem-solving is expected?
- Are the characteristics of the learners being considered?

- Do the methods and media provide variety and encourage learning?

- What is the quality and readability of handouts, computer-based training material and training aids?

Evaluative feedback

- How is progress being assessed during the programme?

- Is each assessment method reliable and timely?

- How is feedback given to the trainees?

- How is feedback used by the tutors? Is there enough flexibility to allow for its use?

EVALUATING THE TRAINING PROCESS

Recent work by psychologists interested in training (for instance, that summarised in Kraiger 2002) has given a much clearer picture of what an ideal training process might look like. Some of this work has been referred to in the earlier chapters, but it seems worthwhile collecting it all into one place so that those who have responsibility for training activities can use it as a benchmark against which to evaluate actual practice.

Figure 8.1 is a simple model that can be used for looking at the whole training process, stage by stage. We shall use each stage of it to summarise what appears to be best practice, given the present level of knowledge.

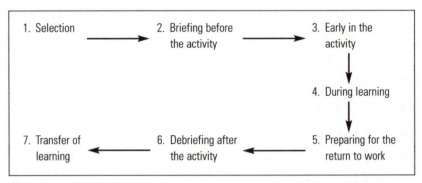

Figure 8.1: The process of training

1. Selection

The important aspect to remember here is that if the wrong person attends the training, there is either no learning or no transfer back to the workplace, ie there is no return on investment.

A useful concept is *just-in-time'* (JIT) training; the person who is to receive training can use the new knowledge and skills very soon after the training activities. The best evidence to support this view comes from research into learning on simulators for flying aircraft. These are sophisticated learning devices and allow the measurement of rate and quality of learning. They can also be used to discover the rate of forgetting over time. The evidence from this research shows that people who have learned knowledge procedures, like the steps necessary in a particular emergency and the sequence in which to carry them out, forget parts of them within weeks if they have not practised them. Procedures that also have a skills component take longer to decay, probably because the learning is richer in the sense of using more senses.

Revision sessions, where the level of performance is reinstated, are necessary when the procedures are not being used. These findings have far-reaching implications for the kind of programme that covers technical or functional knowledge, which all people who have reached a particular level in a part of the organisation attend, regardless of whether they will use the information this year or next. Some will not be able to use the information in the short term and they will forget it. If the programme is to be of value, these people will need detailed notes and check-sheets to refer to and thus refresh their knowledge when use of it is required or, perhaps, access to e-learning or CBL packages that are designed for revision purposes.

Another useful concept is that of the *trainee specification,* ie what kind of person has the necessary skills, knowledge and experience to benefit from the activities being offered. If the specification is accurately defined, the assessment can be made by testing knowledge, skills or aptitude. It might also be necessary to consider whether the experience of the likely delegate has produced a cognitive framework, a way of thinking that suggests that he or she will benefit. For instance, I remember some years ago listening to a lecture by Mintzberg in which he said that he was no longer willing to teach MBA students at Harvard. They were young and recent graduates in business studies and had very little experience in organisations. His view was that they had no framework for understanding organisational contexts and thus could not discuss what, for him, were the important issues.

Research on the transfer of training suggests that high job involvement and self-selection for training may be important as they provide a good deal of motivation to learn and to transfer the learning back to the workplace. An important factor here is 'self-efficacy', which was discussed in Chapter 6. This attitude is a good predictor of learning and of transfer behaviour, and it could be assessed as part of the selection procedure.

Another concept that was mentioned above (in Chapter 5 on changes in skills) is that of 'trainability testing'. For some types of training it is possible to set up a simple selection test and assess whether the proposed delegate can easily learn what is to be offered. For instance, the programme for teaching policemen who wished to join the traffic branch to drive fast cars safely was very long and expensive. It was found to be much more economic to introduce a selection system and then to train, on a much shorter course, only those who were already able to drive quickly and safely. Something similar could be introduced for many of the situations in organisations where employees have to be moved to other parts of the organisation because their particular section is being closed down. The strength of trainability testing is that it allows a realistic self-appraisal of whether the type of work is acceptable, as well as a measure of experience and aptitude.

2 Briefing before the activity

The most important aspect in this stage is that of building up the motivation to learn something during the activity.

Some form of interview is recommended, where the supervisor/line manager discusses with the delegate the reasons for attending the learning activities. This should clarify, for both, what the expectations are, what should be brought back and how it might be used. Sometimes one of the trainers will attend this briefing and this should ensure that all are parties to the learning contract that is being established.

Another aspect of briefing is that it establishes objectives. There is a considerable body of research on setting objectives, and it is clear that they motivate people to learn and to apply the learning. They are also associated with levels of performance and over a considerable range of difficulty they have been shown to be good predictors, ie the higher the difficulty of the goal, the higher the performance (Locke and Latham 1990). The research has also shown that specific goals are much more effective that general exhortation ('do your best' etc). Where the relationship between level of objective and level of performance breaks down, it is usually because the performer is not committed to achieving the task.

One other aspect of pre-briefing that should be noted, as it may be more important than the others, is that it involves the supervisor/line manager 'buying-in' to the training. It sets up the expectation that some useful learning will occur and that this can be of value to the particular part of the organisation. This helps to set the 'climate for transfer', which was discussed in Chapter 7 on evaluating before planning a training activity. Without a positive climate for transfer, much of the time spent on learning will be wasted as the new knowledge and skills will not be applied in the workplace.

3 Early in the activity

The key aspect in this stage of the process is to encourage the desire to learn what is on offer. Without this motivation, much of the time will be wasted.

Where the pre-briefing has been done thoroughly, as described above, much of this will already have been done. The delegates will be committed to a set of objectives and be clear about what they are expecting to learn and what they are expected to bring back to the workplace. Where this has not happened, the first part of the programme will be to establish these goals and objectives. Essentially, the process should bring into line the objectives of the trainees, the trainers and the line managers. There is a danger here that the objectives set at the beginning of the programme may not be as accurate a reflection of the work requirement as those set in a pre-briefing session. Sometimes one sees at the beginning of programmes, particularly those concerned with interpersonal relationships, objectives on flip charts that are at a high level of generality and which have little obvious connection to work. Such objectives are unlikely to provide the focus and motivation associated with specific goals formulated to achieve high levels of performance (Locke and Latham 1990).

A second aspect of encouraging the delegates to put themselves into a learning position is to treat them like adults. Historically, most technical training has been based upon pedagogical ideas derived from education, ie the teacher knows and by demonstration and exhortation teaches the learner (who is assumed not to know). This model works quite well with young children but it does not work at all well with teenagers and is inappropriate for most adult learning situations. Adults have a past, they have experience, and they learn best by bringing in their experience and, through reflection, analysing it. In Chapter 7 we discussed a cycle of learning (Kolb 1984), based upon the idea of bringing in experience and developing ideas on what might work better, and there is also a considerable literature on adult learning, which can help (Knowles 1984). There should also be an element here of using opportunities, early in the activity, to focus on the utility of the learning and to make the learning situations realistic. There is much evidence that these are important to adults in fostering the motivation to learn.

In Chapter 6, when we were discussing changes in attitudes, the concept of 'self-efficacy' was introduced. This is a perception of being confident to carry out a planned task successfully. It is a good predictor of learning and a very good predictor of transfer of learning back to the workplace (Stajkovic and Luthans 1998). However, 'being confident' requires a realistic assessment of the situation in which the task is to be performed (whether in the learning activity or the workplace). Often the ability to perform it under 'safe' conditions in the training centre is not the same as having to do it in the workplace. It is worthwhile looking at the concept in greater detail as it might well be a crucial factor in effective training. Sources of self-efficacy have been shown to be:

- Performance accomplishments: actually doing the task, where necessary in steps graded from 'safe' modelling through to full performance.

- Vicarious experience: learning by watching others, particularly through the observation of many successful models.

- Verbal persuasion: accepting the view of someone thought to have expertise, who insists that the task can be done well. With adults this is not nearly as powerful as the preceding two sources.

An important question for us, when thinking about the design of learning situations is, 'What can we do to increase the level of self-efficacy?' The literature (Stajkovic and Luthans 1998; Mathieu, Martineau et al 1993) suggests a number of areas that should be considered:

- How can we maximize the similarity between the training situation and the job? Is it necessary to carry out the training in phases interspersed with job experience in order to provide a realistic, informed view of the likely situation in which the learning is to be applied?

- How can we provide a wide range of experience of what is being learned so that the principles can be applied to situations that are rather different from those simulated in the learning situation?

- To what extent can realistic goals be set? Goal-setting will be important because without it the learners will have a poor basis for judging their progress. Clear measures of progress are essential for increasing self-efficacy. Trainees should be deterred from setting very difficult goals, as those who give up are often those who self-impose very high standards and then feel no sense of accomplishment when they fail to achieve them.

- How can we ensure that what is being learned will be supported and rewarded in the workplace? To what extent must the supervisor or manager be involved in the learning process?

4. During learning

The key idea here is that high-quality learning is more likely to transfer. How then does the literature define high-quality learning?

One way is to think in terms of matching the training process with the task. For instance, the training of supervisors on aspects of their jobs like conflict management, relationships with staff, or relationships with customers. As a tutor on a workshop, one can explain what the organisation believes is good practice and show a few video-tape demonstrations of this acted out. This is essentially learning of cognitive procedures, chains of desirable actions. However, these parts of the job are actually skills, and high-quality learning should include the performance of them and feedback for each supervisor. A landmark study (Latham and Saari 1979) showed how to produce high-quality learning in these kinds of tasks. The supervisors were taken off-job for a couple of hours every other week and encouraged to bring in problems that they had had with key results areas, such as motivating a poor performer, dealing with discrimination complaints, conducting a performance review, giving on-the-job training, etc. The situations were role-played by the person bringing in the problem and another delegate. Discussion of this role-play and other ways of handling similar situations drew out the important learning points. The supervisors returned to work and some were faced with situations similar to those role-played. At the next training workshop, a couple of weeks later, some were able to describe how they had tackled such situations after the first workshop and how successful their approach had been; then a new problem area was role-played and discussed. There are great theoretical strengths to this approach:

■ It matches the learning situation to the task.

■ It uses examples brought in by the supervisors and is thus based upon their experience.

■ It allows for the practising of a skill and the observation of others using similar skills (both contributing to self-efficacy).

■ It uses the whole cycle of experience, reflection, thinking about it and trying a new way of solving the problem. It also goes around this cycle a number of times.

It is not surprising that the training approach was very successful in changing the behaviour of the supervisors and contributing to greater effectiveness.

In the chapters above dealing with evaluating knowledge and skills learning, it was pointed out that a number of levels could be identified. For knowledge, these were:

■ declarative knowledge, 'knowing what'

■ procedural knowledge, 'knowing 'how'

■ analysis and decision-making, 'knowing which, when and why'.

It should be clear that high-quality learning can result only if the desired level for performance is learned during the training. One should not expect people to be able to analyse situations and select appropriate procedures if they have not actually practised this in a number of situations.

With skills learning, there are two possible approaches. The first is called the 'identical elements' approach – the replication of the work task as accurately as possible in training so that most of the elements of the task are represented. This leads to 'over-learning' and the ability to produce high-level performance even when other things are going on. An example is that of driving a motor car while listening to the radio and carrying on a conversation. This kind of learning can, however, be dysfunctional as it is difficult to change, should that be necessary. The second approach is the learning of principles. The principles are learned by the examination of a number of examples, with some variation so that similarities can be identified. The later use of principles, as opposed to stereotyped behaviour, allows for more flexibility, as the learned behaviour can be modified in different situations and can be developed to cope with new situations.

The research literature on learning shows that there is an interesting dilemma for trainers who are interested in providing high-quality training. People learn more quickly and enjoyably when the material is structured for them so that they can progress through levels of difficulty, carefully graduated to take them from their starting level of ability smoothly up to higher levels. However, when they have to struggle to understand, when they find something difficult to learn (but succeed through persistence) it is often the case that they value the experience more and retain the learning much longer. Learning that has been difficult to achieve transfers much better than that which has been easy (Hesketh 1997). This poses a problem for trainers. Should they structure the learning opportunities so that delegates learn quickly and enjoy the process, or should they allow the situations to become difficult and let the learners struggle?

Perhaps there is a more general principle here. How many attentive and well-meaning parents do you know who have provided everything for their children and whose children are unable to succeed in, or even cope with, adult life? How many people do you know whose parents were unable to provide much help, but who have been successful because they felt that it was up to them to overcome adversity and do it for themselves. I think that it was Bill Shankley (hugely successful manager of Liverpool Football Club) who said, 'I didn't have any education, I had to use my own brains'.

Another aspect of this dilemma is that evaluation at the end of training – how much they learned, how much of it they thought would be useful, how much they enjoyed themselves – is not a good predictor of how much of the learning they will later use. There is a good deal of research evidence to support this opinion (Alliger and Janak 1989; Alliger, Tannenbaum et el 1997).

One other issue that is worth considering under this heading of what should happen during the learning activity, is that of 'spaced' versus 'massed' practice. Many of us are familiar with the massed practice provided by revision shortly before an examination. This enables high performance on the day, but the accumulated knowledge is rather rapidly forgotten. A small amount of revision, at intervals during the year, spaces the practice out and leads to more effective learning in the sense that it is retained for longer.

5. Preparing for the return to work

The emphasis during this stage of the training process is on facilitating transfer of the learning to the work. Central to this is an emphasis on the utility of the learning throughout the training activity.

Earlier in this chapter (pp. 109–10), a method was described for reviewing progress, thinking about what had been learned, and thinking about how this learning might be used. Some such procedure should be part of most training activities.

The focus on utility and identification of which pieces of learning are particularly useful leads directly to the construction of an 'action plan' (pp. 110–11). This again taps into the motivation and performance associated with goal setting (Locke and Latham 1990) and the more specific the actions listed, the better. The action plan should list a set of goals for up to six months after the programme. A longer timeframe is usually unrealistic, as events within the organisation are likely to overtake such plans. Similarly, a large number of actions is likely to be unrealistic. Some force-field analysis should be done for each action with an indication of what and who might help, and what or who might hinder. Usually the first action listed will be to discuss the action plan and agree the actions with the line manager. Without the support of such a person, it is unlikely that a positive climate for transfer will exist. The requirements for a positive climate were described on page 91.

A more precise view of what the action planning process might include is provided by the work on 'relapse prevention'. This concept was actually developed to support medical treatments for addictions and obesity – situations where the person undergoing treatment would be likely to give it up when under some pressure. The work has been adapted to support management development activities (Marx 1986) and it would suggest that the trainees should actively prepare for the organisational situation to which they expect to return, by:

■ setting specific and challenging goals

■ anticipating the difficulties of using the new approaches in the workplace

■ predicting the circumstances in which these difficulties will arise

- role-playing or discussing likely difficult situations in order to develop coping responses

- specific problem-solving practice so that potentially high-risk situations can be treated as challenges

- developing coping strategies to avoid the feelings of guilt from early failure to apply the new procedures successfully

- work out ways of retaining the new skills over time

- identify sources of support (self-reward, 'buddy' agreements, etc)

- actively monitor progress on achieving the goals set.

6. Debriefing after the activity and transfer of learning

If the first five phases in Figure 8.1 have been done properly then it should be possible to return to work and transfer the learning. However, often the learning 'burns off' on re-entry because no one in the workplace carries out a debriefing and/or offers support and encouragement. The most common experience is to be greeted by, 'Had a good time? We have been busy while you have been away but we have kept some of it for you and it's all in your in-tray'.

In the CIPD 2003 survey, a quarter of the organisations reported on said that employees 'always' got an opportunity to discuss action plans with their line managers. A further 55 per cent reported that such written statements were 'sometimes' the subject of discussion at debriefing sessions. Trainers reported that line managers in their organisations were generally positive towards training and development, but often did not support them effectively. The figures for following-up training programmes were:

Level of involvement	% of trainers agreeing
Always sufficiently involved	12
Could be slightly more involved	37
Could be a lot more involved	47
Not involved at all	4

There seems to be a good deal of room for improvement here.

In the debriefing by the supervisor or line manager, the objectives etc in the action plan should be agreed. There should be some encouragement to apply the learning in situations of the learner's own choosing, and there should be some linking back to the briefing before the activity. All of this contributes to the 'opportunity' part on the performance equation described on p. 89.

If the activity has been well run, and 'self-efficacy' has been built up, there will be a good deal of (intrinsic) self-motivation to perform using the new learning. The 'motivation' aspect of the equation also implies the provision of some sort of extrinsic reward, such as better assignments, different tasking, recognition of the new skills, perhaps the chance to train others. Many of the factors involved in producing a positive 'climate for transfer' (which was discussed above on p. 91) will also be necessary to contribute towards the motivation to use the learning.

IN BRIEF

Evaluation during a learning activity can be a useful source of information with which to improve the quality of the event.

One aspect that is worth considering is the clarification of the objectives so that there is a shared understanding of what the learners and the tutors are trying to achieve. Some method of relating the objectives to organisational goals should also be established. Methods for achieving this link are described in Chapter 2.

Reviewing the progress of the learning during the event is an extension of the process of establishing shared objectives. A focus on the *utility* of the learning, and action planning for application of it in the workplace, will reinforce the link between objectives for the event and organisational requirements.

Information gathered by questionnaire at the end of a learning event is too late to be useful for improving the quality of the activities that have already been run. If the information is to be used to improve the quality of future events, very careful selection of questions is necessary. It will also be necessary to justify the belief that the next set of participants will require the same learning experience in order to achieve their objectives.

General questions and overall ratings are of little value for the purpose of 'feedback' on the quality of the course. These ratings are subject to many sources of bias and do not predict either the amount of learning or the likelihood of future behaviour change. Where the interest is in the performance of the tutors, a better source of information is a checklist of behaviour, such as that in Table 5.1.

Where the interest is in the programme as a whole, some comparison of it against the ideal given by the criteria listed above, under evaluating the training process, should provide the relevant data.

◼ REFERENCES AND FURTHER READING

ALLIGER G.M. *and* JANAK E.A. (1989) 'Kirkpatrick's levels of training criteria: thirty years later'. *Personnel Psychology 42.* 331–342.

ALLIGER G.M., TANNENBAUM S.I., BENNET W. et al (1997) 'A meta-analysis of the relations among training criteria'. *Personnel Psychology, 50.* 341–358.

BRAMLEY P. (1994) *Using Subordinate Appraisals as Feedback.* Paper given to the 23rd International Congress of Applied Psychology. Madrid.

BRAMLEY P. *and* HULLAH H. (1987) 'Auditing Training'. *Journal of European Industrial Training 11.* 6, 5–10.

CIPD (2003) *Training and Development 2003.* London, CIPD.

HMSO (1989) *Training in Britain: A Study of Funding, Activity and Attitudes.* London, HMSO.

HESKETH B. (1997) 'Dilemmas in Training for Transfer and Retention'. *Applied Psychology: An International Review.* 46, (4), 317–386.

KNOWLES M. (1984) *The Adult Learner: A Neglected Species.* Houston (Texas), The Gulf Publishing Company.

KOLB D.A. (1984) *Experiential Learning.* Englewood Cliffs, NY, Prentice-Hall.

KRAIGER K. (ed) (2002) *Creating, implementing and maintaining effective training and development: State-of-the-art lessons for practice.* San Francisco, Jossey-Bass.

LATHAM G.P. *and* SAARI L.M. (1979) 'The application of Social Learning Theory to training supervisors through behavioural modelling'. *Journal of Applied Psychology.* 64, 239–246.

LOCKE E.A. *and* LATHAM G.P. (1990) *A Theory of Goal Setting and Task Performance.* Englewood Cliffs, NJ, Prentice-Hall.

MARX R.D. (1986) 'Improving management development through relapse prevention strategies'. *Journal of Management Development.* 5, 27–40.

MATHIEU J.E., MARTINEAU J.W. *and* TANNEBAUM S.I. (1993) 'Individual and situational influences on the development of self-efficacy; Implications for training effectiveness'. *Personnel Psychology.* 46, 125–147.

RALPHS L.T. *and* STEPHAN E. (1986) 'HRD in the Fortune 500'. *Training and Development Journal.* 40, 69–76.

STAJKOVIC A.D. *and* LUTHANS F. (1998) 'Self-efficacy and Work-related Performance: A Meta-analysis'. *Psychological Bulletin.* 124, 2, 240–261.

9 ▪ THE END-GAME

Previous chapters of the book have each ended with a summary of the main ideas, and it is not the intention to repeat those here. In this final chapter some more general issues will be discussed. These are: reporting on evaluations, ensuring that the findings are used, ethical issues and the whole political arena that surrounds evaluation. There is also a blueprint for good practice – the Investors in People initiative.

PRESENTING AN EVALUATION REPORT

The final stage of most evaluations will be the presentation of a report. The extent to which this will be accepted and acted upon will depend, to a large extent, on what took place at the beginning of the study. It is crucial to identify the major stakeholders and to try to discover what agendas they have. Sensitivity to the conflicting aims and interests can be enhanced by discussing with a number of stakeholders what data should be collected. Many of those who have a long-term interest in the programme will have strong views on the desired outcomes of the study. It is essential to keep such people informed during the evaluation, and to involve them in key decisions if they are to 'own' and therefore act on the results. This is not to imply that the evaluator must produce the findings that they are expecting, rather that their views must be incorporated and they must be kept informed. It is, of course, also essential to establish that the people receiving the report have the power to implement the changes being suggested.

One way of overcoming some of the problems in presenting the report is to discover what kind of report the major stakeholders expect. In the section on measuring changes in attitudes, a series of alternative approaches to evaluation was given in Table 6.2, an extract of which is shown below.

	Evaluation of training *should* be:	
Statistical and scientific, as its primary concern is with objective measurement	1 2 3 4 5 6 7	Anecdotal and descriptive, as its primary concern is with subjective interpretation
A carefully planned process with a set agenda	1 2 3 4 5 6 7	Changing throughout as the focus changes during the process
Estimating the worth of training activities to the organisation	1 2 3 5 6 7	Providing feedback to the training department
Based on large samples and asking quite simple questions	1 2 3 4 5 6 7	Based on small samples and using in-depth questioning

Making a decision on each of the alternatives in this table makes explicit what kind of process evaluation is thought to be. I suggest that, before embarking on an evaluation, you ask the major stakeholders to fill in a set of attitude scales like those in Table 6.2. You will then know what kind of data they think that you ought to collect, and something about how they expect you to present it. That should at least alert you to some of the problems if their views are very different to your own. In most cases, I think that it will also assist the process of putting the case and helping them to make changes.

The nature of the report will, of course, reflect the purpose for which it is written, but generally it will contain most of the following sections:

■ a summary, which is intended for those who will not have time to read the full report. Care should be taken to ensure that this is a balanced extract, as many people will not read (or remember) the supporting arguments in the main body of the report

■ a statement of the purpose of the evaluation and how it was designed to meet that purpose

■ a description of the methods used for data collection and a summary of the findings

■ a summary of costs

■ the resulting outputs from the activities expressed in terms of increased individual and organisational benefits – both 'pay back' and 'pay forward'

- conclusions drawn from previous sections. These may sometimes be recommendations if the purpose of the evaluation requires these.

The way in which the findings are communicated during the study will depend upon the organisational style. Some organisations prefer written memoranda, but in many the important decisions are actually made in face-to-face discussions. Discussion of what is emerging from the data often leads to a greater sense of shared responsibility and thus a willingness to accept the results as being valid. The presentation of the report itself is not the time to 'defend'. If there is some bad news, those concerned should be aware of it before the presentation. At the very least, this allows them to say that they are aware of some problems and have started to do something about them, rather than provoking a defensive reaction.

An evaluation report will usually be part of a change process, and it is helpful to consider the method of change which is to be used. The literature on planned organisational change can help here, as a number of such models for this process have been described.

One possible method is to consider the process as one of *research followed by dissemination* of the findings. The underlying philosophy of this is that as the research has been carefully carried out, the target audience will accept it and act to carry out the changes suggested. The recipients of the report are expected to agree that the study is valid, accept its conclusions, see the importance of the changes being recommended, and be willing to make them. This is a popular method in large organisations where surveys are carried out and the findings are widely disseminated. However, it often has very little effect because the target population considers the findings to be merely information rather than a basis for action.

A second possibility is to think of the process as one of *social interaction*. The recipients of the report are seen as holding a variety of views and positions with respect to the activity being evaluated, and are therefore likely to adopt different attitudes and responses to the findings. Using an approach which is sensitive to this implies that it is necessary to make face-to-face contacts with different audiences, and thus the process is nearer to one of negotiation than one of simple dissemination of information.

A third plausible method is to treat the process as one of *planned change*. Here data collection and research is shared between the evaluator and the clients, usually line managers. Information is considered useful only if it leads to action. The assumption is that change occurs through a continuous process of data generation (where are we now?), planning (where do we want to be?) and implementation (what should we do next?). The changes being introduced need to be supported so that they are utilised and become part of everyday routines; this can be done only by the clients.

The purpose of the evaluation will vary and the process will differ in different organisations. What I am suggesting is that you should think about the process and ask yourself the following questions:

■ Are you intending to produce conclusions or achieve change?

■ What sort of target audience do you have? Are they relatively passive and likely to accept the changes? Do the changes need to be negotiated?

■ When do you withdraw from the scene? Should you continue to be involved as a change agent would be until the changes have become part of the routine?

Whatever method is adopted, a successful presentation of a report should result in action planning by the recipients. An effective report must contain information that recipients will find meaningful, as they are unlikely to introduce changes if they cannot understand the data or do not find them relevant to their problems. The information should also have some impact so that it can energise some change and be a stimulus to further action or investigation. This may often mean a clear statement that something is wrong and that it needs attention. It may also mean that suggestions about how to change the status quo will be necessary in order to overcome inertia. It is worth emphasising again that the report should be presented to those who have the ability to make the necessary changes.

UTILISATION OF FINDINGS

An evaluation is carried out to meet a purpose, and one might argue that the work is only worthwhile if the findings are *used*. Four aspects might have an important effect on utilisation (Levinton and Hughes 1981):

■ relevance of the findings to decisions that have to be made

■ communication between researchers and users

■ plausibility of the research results

■ user involvement in the evaluation.

For instance, collecting the data is only one part of the feedback process; the trainers also have to receive it and act on it. They need to be convinced of the accuracy of the findings and of the need for the changes proposed. This almost always implies that they should be involved in collecting and analysing the data.

The literature also suggests guidelines for increasing the likelihood of the findings being utilised (Patton 1997):

- Try to understand how the key decision-makers think. For instance, there is no point in presenting complex statistical analysis to a 'politician', but it might be necessary if you are trying to convince a scientist.

- Oral presentations and answering questions will usually be more appropriate than long papers.

- Wide participation in the design process increases sensitivity to the varied interests of the main stakeholders and makes them part of the evaluation.

However careful and scientific the collection of data, it is often useful to think of evaluation as a political process. Perhaps the best book on the subject is that by Patton (1997) and his research has shown that scientific validity (whether other researchers think that the study accords with sound scientific principles) is often far less important than face validity (for instance, whether the information sources are thought to be reliable, or whether key power brokers have been involved) when estimating the degree to which evaluative findings will be used.

Objectivity of evaluation

It should be obvious from a consideration of the various strategies available that an evaluation will never produce *the* truth. Some approaches collect relatively hard data which can be reliably measured, but the evaluators will hold values that determine which information will be collected and what evidence will be considered acceptable. Some approaches involve a wide range of stakeholders and attempt to get at a *wider* truth by looking for consensus.

The objectivity within an evaluation comes from a conviction that if someone else had carried out the study he or she would have come to the similar conclusions. As my old professor, Alec Rodger, used to say, 'A study should be technically sound, administratively convenient and politically defensible'. The evaluation will rarely be objective in the scientific sense of a passive observation of events. Usually the presence of the evaluator will change perceptions of some people about whatever is being investigated and thus it is, to some extent, a political activity.

ETHICAL ISSUES

One aspect of this political flavour of evaluation is that ethical issues are often raised. An interesting, if rather elderly, study (Morris and Cohn 1993) reported the findings of a survey of 456 professional evaluators who were asked whether they had encountered any ethical problems in their work[3]. If the answer to this question was 'yes', each respondent was asked to describe the three most frequent and the one most serious problem. Problems rated as 'frequent' included:

- The stakeholder had already decided what the findings should be and was only using the evaluation to strengthen his position (reported by 55% of the respondents).
- The evaluator was pressured by a stakeholder to alter findings (62%).
- Findings were either suppressed or ignored (32%).
- Findings were used to punish someone (16%).
- Findings were used to punish the evaluator (10%).

There was also the interesting finding that those who had experienced ethical problems were mainly external evaluators. Those who spent most of their time on internal evaluations tended to report not having faced ethical problems. It seems unlikely that internal evaluations involve fewer ethical problems than external ones, and the authors argue that it is more likely that internals are so close to the stakeholders that they do not recognise the ethical issues.

The survey is an old one but, in my experience, things haven't changed much in the past 10 years. Evaluating something that someone else really cares about can be a difficult process.

INVESTORS IN PEOPLE

While thinking of political aspects of evaluation we might look at the 'big P' intervention, the British Government initiative, Investors in People. Successive governments in the UK have tried to encourage organisations to spend more time and money on training and development of their people. However, most of these initiatives have been intended to increase funding for technical education in the belief that a better qualified workforce will be more productive. Employers, by and large, have agreed with this, but have been reluctant to invest their own money in it. Evaluation of work placement schemes, sponsored by central government, have often shown that employers were not actually very interested in the skills possessed by those on placement, but were using the scheme to recruit youngsters with positive attitudes (Bramley and Carruthers 1986). The IiP initiative, introduced in 1990, is a very different kind of intervention. It has the aim of creating a benchmark to encourage organisations to improve the effectiveness of their training and development activities by linking them with criteria of organisational effectiveness. In the year 2000, some 40,000 organisations in the UK were involved in IiP; about half had achieved the IiP accreditation and the other half were formally committed to the process and hoped to be accredited in due course (IRS 2000).

The IiP standard includes four principles, and a number of indicators are used to assess whether the organisation has met the requirements. A summary of these is given below:

Commitment. To invest in people to achieve business goals. Indicators include:

- The organisation is committed to supporting the development of its people.

- People are encouraged to improve their own and other people's performance.

- People believe that their contribution to the organisation is recognised.

Planning. How skills, individuals and teams are developed to achieve these business goals. Indicators include:

- The organisation has a plan with clear aims and objectives that are understood by everyone.

- The development of people is in line with the organisation's aims and objectives.

- People understand how they contribute to achieving the organisation's aims and objectives.

Action. To develop and use necessary skills in a well-designed and continuing programme directly tied to business objectives. Indicators include:

- Managers are effective in supporting the development of people.

- People learn and develop effectively.

Evaluating outcomes of training and development for individuals' progress towards goals, the value achieved and future needs.

- The development of people improves the performance of the organisation, team and individuals.

- People understand the impact of the development of people on the performance of the organisation, teams and individuals.

- The organisation gets better at developing its people.

It is clear that this standard implies a move towards what we called 'strategic training' in Chapter 1, and should result in linking training investment with the development of the organisation. It should also be obvious that it is a charter for evaluators, requiring them to demonstrate the links between developing people and various forms of effectiveness. However, to date, few of them seem to have taken up the challenge.

For instance, the IRS (2000) survey of 79 organisations concluded that, 'there is no body of evidence to demonstrate the connection between effective training and business performance'. Those who have read this book carefully must surely feel that, if this is the case, the wrong questions have been asked. As we know only too well, it is not easy to establish the connection between training and aspects of effectiveness, but it can be done. Asking employers simple questions, long after the training has taken place, in large-scale survey work is not the way to do it. A better approach was used by Downs and Smith (1997) in their detailed qualitative investigation of 10 organisations which had achieved IiP status. Almost all of the organisations in their study stated initially that there was no discernible benefit in business performance. However, this view of 'business performance' proved to be very simplistic, and during further discussions almost all of the organisations identified benefits that could be measured and that we would identify as fitting into the criteria of organisational effectiveness discussed in Chapter 2. This is closer to what we might expect.

As we know, having read this book carefully, a better approach would be to use the model of training shown in Figure 1.2 (p. 6), ie

- Identify what aspects of effectiveness or performance are to be changed.

- Decide how the levels of these are to be measured.

- Isolate the behaviours necessary to achieve the desired levels.

- Then intervene with developmental activities and changes to the organisational context that will support the learning.

It would then be possible to evaluate the impact of the developmental activities in terms of increased effectiveness and improved performance.

IN CONCLUSION

There has never been greater pressure to evaluate training and developmental activities.

- The IiP initiative requires that 'People understand the impact of the development of people on the performance of the organisation, teams and individuals'. The implication of this is that most activities should be evaluated and the impact of them in terms of pay-back and pay-forward should be assessed.

- The move towards strategic training, linking training with the strategic plans of the organisation, also implies sophisticated evaluation. Senior managers think that 'linking training to performance' and 'evaluating cost-effective training' are issues that are very important to their organisations (CIPD 2000).

- The CIPD 2003 report suggests that training is increasingly being delivered with the aim of solving specific organisational problems, and that making the case for training implies making a *business* case for it. This must imply assessing the impact of training *before* the event as well as after.

- There is a large increase in the supply of training by electronic means, often from external providers. If this is not to become an expensive fad for demonstrating how up to date the training function is, the packages need to be carefully assessed for suitability to the target population and the organisational requirement. This is not merely a matter of testing learning; there must also be some system for monitoring the effectiveness of the whole process and the application of the learning.

Many of the readers of this book will be providers of training, either directly or because responsibility for training is a significant part of their jobs. For such people there is an important political aspect to evaluation. To gain influence in the organisation, the training function needs to pay attention to four main areas:

- Other departments must really want what the training department has to offer.

- The activities carried out should be those not easily performed by others inside or outside the organisation.

- The activities carried out should be clearly related to the achievement of high-priority organisational goals.

- The activities should be evaluated and show a positive return on investment.

If this is to happen, the training manager must be involved with the policy-making groups and be in close contact with senior line managers. The argument then comes full circle because such people can identify the key strategic initiatives and training activities can be built around them.

Training functions have traditionally been expected to provide well-designed courses and have gained respect by ensuring good attendance on such courses and good trainee reactions to them. This is a politically naïve position. A much stronger position has been achieved by training managers who have set up alliances and coalitions to achieve some influence (Sloman 1998). Good practice in this respect includes:

- written explicit training plans often linked to a broader programme of change within the organisation

- regular written reports to the board, and feedback from line managers on the impact and relevance of training

- a clear link between performance management and the identification of training needs

- widespread evaluation of the impact of training events

- tighter management of the training function, leading to a much sharper focus.

Chapter 7 of this book, describing how to evaluate *before* designing a learning event, and Chapter 2, which describes how to identify and measure changes in effectiveness should provide a lot of ideas on how all this can be done.

Getting into the faraway parts of the organisation and evaluating the impact of activities on criteria of effectiveness is something of an adventure. My intention in writing this book has been to provide a guide for the adventurous traveller. Perhaps it is also appropriate to wish all such travellers good luck and to hope that they will survive and prosper.

REFERENCES AND FURTHER READING

BRAMLEY P. *and* CARRUTHERS L. (1986) '*An evaluation of the work placement scheme in the Docklands'*. Unpublished report to the Docklands Development Board.

CIPD (2000) *Training and Development in Britain 2000*. London, CIPD.

CIPD (2003) *Training and Development in Britain 2003*. London, CIPD.

DOWNS S. *and* SMITH D. (1997) 'It pays to be nice to people. Investors in people: The search for measurable benefits'. *Personnel Review*. 27, 2, 143–155.

IRS (2000) 'Investors in People: More process than profit'. *IRS Employment Review*. 708, 5–16.

LEVITON L.C. *and* HUGHES E.F.X. (1981) 'Research on the utilization of evaluations: A review and synthesis'. *Evaluation Review*. 5, 525–548.

[3]MORRIS M. *and* COHN R. (1993) 'Programme evaluators and ethical challenges: A national survey'. *Evaluation Review*. 17, 6, 621–642.

PATTON M.Q. (1997) *Utilization focussed evaluation*. Beverley Hills, Sage.

SLOMAN M. (1998) *A Handbook of Training Strategy (2nd ed)* Aldershot, Gower.

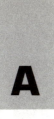

A ■ APPENDIX: RELIABILITY OF TESTING

Reliability of testing is an important issue but, within the field of training, one that is largely neglected. Many of the short tests that are used to assess learning are not reliable measures. Unreliable measures will produce estimates of knowledge or skills that may look precise but will be misleading. For instance, imagine yourself in the situation of trying, by use of tests, to grade 100 young job applicants into the following proportions:

A	B	C	D	E
10%	20%	40%	20%	10%

Your intention is to offer jobs to the top 30 per cent and put the next 40 per cent on to a waiting-list.

If you did the grading on the basis of height, and you measured the height of each one carefully, you could expect to allocate the tallest 10 to grade A, the next 20 to grade B and so on. One or two might be in the wrong grade because of some 'human error' of measurement. This would imply some unreliability in the testing situation – 'to err is human' – but there should be very little of it. (You would, of course, find yourself in some difficulty about proving the suitability of the test for the purpose, ie its *validity*. It seems certain that someone would ask you to prove this, as the test would discriminate against female candidates.)

Height was chosen as an example of a measure that is reliable. It is, however, rarely an important criterion in job selection. But suppose that you work in the financial sector and that the jobs entail a good deal of numerical work. You set the applicants a test of one hundred short questions on arithmetic. How much unreliability would you expect? How many candidates do you think would be allocated to the wrong grades because of unreliability of the testing situation? The answer might surprise you, as it would probably be about 20 per cent of them. Why should this be?

- You are sampling their knowledge by using only a hundred questions to estimate their total knowledge. This is a source of unreliability because the actual questions asked will suit some of them better than others.

- People tend to perform better on some days than on others. Are you measuring the best that they can do or something much lower than that because they are not well, or overtired?

- Some people perform better early in the morning and others do not really wake up until later in the day.

- Some people are really motivated by test situations and rise to the challenge; others find that test situations make them anxious and they underperform.

- Some errors will be made in the scoring.

This inevitable unreliability in the testing situation is the main reason why selection at eleven-plus for grammar school education became indefensible. It was (and is) impossible to pick out the top 20 per cent and not get some youngsters on the wrong side of the decision line. If the tests are used to stream them into three or four classes in the same school the mistakes are not so serious, as they can be rectified during the year by careful monitoring of performance. If the test results are used to allocate the young people to different schools then it is very difficult to correct the mistaken decisions.

It must surely be important to establish that measures are reliable if important decisions are to be made on the basis of test results. Tests that have low reliability are providing incorrect information, and this is useless for the purpose of making good decisions.

ESTIMATING TEST RELIABILITY

Reliability can be estimated and expressed as a figure that runs from zero (no reliability) to 1 (completely reliable). In the example of trying to allocate 100 people to five grades, different levels of reliability will give the following proportions of people who will be wrongly graded:

Reliability	=	1.0	Wrongly graded	=	0%
	=	0.9		=	23%
	=	0.8		=	33%
	=	0.7		=	40%
	=	0.5		=	50%

At what level would you say that the test results should be ignored as a source of data for decision-making? I would argue that if the reliability falls below 0.8, the results are, to say the least, misleading.

If a test is reliable it will give consistent results; those who are good will obtain good scores each time they attempt it, and those who are poor will obtain poor marks. The classic way to estimate test reliability is to use the test twice on the same group of candidates. A reliable test will give much the same rank order on each occasion; the same people will be at or near the top, and the candidates who were at or near the bottom on the first test will also be there on the re-test. A good example of a reliable test situation is the one above of measuring height. Measuring the same person a number of times would give very similar results. Where tests are samples of something they will be less reliable, because there is always a problem of estimating the whole from a sample.

Test/retest reliability

Using our example of 100 questions in arithmetic, let us assume that the candidates were tested twice and the results of 20 of them were:

Candidate	A	B	C	D	E	F	G	H	J	K	L	M	N	O	P	Q	R	S	T	U
Test	91	83	76	68	66	64	62	60	59	58	56	56	55	53	52	51	50	49	46	43
Retest	93	86	75	66	60	63	58	68	49	50	58	62	58	40	49	50	41	55	50	46

Plotting the two sets of scores on a scattergram allows us to estimate reliability by eye, and a simple calculation will help us to decide whether the reliability is higher than 0.8, and therefore acceptable, or less than this figure.

First the plots: A has two scores in the 90s and goes into the top right-hand cell. Similarly B with two 80s and C with two 70s. The candidate R has 50 on the test and 41 on the retest ie cell 50+/40+. The full set of plots is shown in Figure A1.

The long cigar shape produced by the plots in Table A1 implies good reliability. High scores on the original test are predicting high scores on the retest. The lower scores are less good predictors but the trend is close to a diagonal line.

To calculate a figure for the reliability of the test we need to correlate the two sets of test scores. There are many ways to do this, and many pocket-size calculators are capable of carrying out the procedure. The simplest way to estimate the reliability is to rearrange the plots into four quadrants:

Test Score	40–	40+	45+	50+	55+	60+	65+	70+	80+	90+
90+										A
80+									B	
70+								C		
65+						E	D			
60+					G	F	H			
55+			J	K	N L	M				
50+		R O	P	Q						
45+				T	S					
40+			U							
40–										
	40–	40+	45+	50+	55+	60+	65+	70+	80+	90+

Retest score

Figure A1: A Scattergram

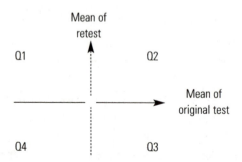

If the testing situation has high reliability, the plots should fall into the quadrants Q2 and Q4, ie high/high or low/low.

The dividing lines for the quadrants are provided by the means (the average scores for the tests). The mean mark of the original test is 59.9, and for the retest it is 58.9. The quadrants are thus:

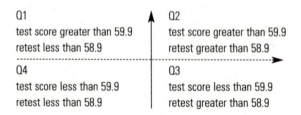

Q1
test score greater than 59.9
retest less than 58.9

Q2
test score greater than 59.9
retest greater than 58.9

Q4
test score less than 59.9
retest less than 58.9

Q3
test score less than 59.9
retest greater than 58.9

Plotting our scores into these four quadrants gives:

	Q1		Q2
	G		A, B, C, D
			E, F, H
59.9			
	Q4		Q3
	J, K, L, N,		M
	O, P, Q, R,		
	S, T, U		
		58.9	

Now we are ready for our simple calculation. Multiply the number of plots in Q2 by those in Q4 and then divide this number by Q1 multiplied by Q3.

$$\frac{Q2 \times Q4}{Q1 \times Q3} = \frac{7 \times 11}{1 \times 1} = \frac{77}{1} = 77$$

This figure of 77 can be compared with those in a simple table to give an estimate of reliability.

Q2 × Q4/Q1 × Q3 =	4	6	8.5	15	21	34	71
Reliability =	0.5	0.6	0.7	0.8	0.85	0.9	0.95

Our testing situation has a reliability of slightly better than 0.95, which is satisfactory. Indeed it is difficult to produce tests of ability that have higher levels of reliability than this.

It should be clear from this example that it is not possible to produce an exact rank order of ability from test results that are samples. We have a reliable testing situation but the estimated rank order on the original test is not the same as that on the retest. It is also very difficult to draw a line and say, 'Candidates who score below this figure will fail.' Suppose we were to decide that 50 was the pass mark, who would 'fail'? On the sample of ability in the 'test', candidates S, T and U. On the sample of ability estimated by the retest, candidates J, O, P, R and U.

Split-half reliability

The test and retest method of establishing reliability is widely used to develop psychometric tests of ability. It is, however, impractical as a procedure for checking the reliability of tests used in training. It is not a sensible use of training time to go through the whole procedure of testing twice. A more practical (although rather less accurate) way of estimating the reliability of a test is to use the 'split-half' method. In this the scores on the odd-numbered items (questions 1, 3, 5, etc) in the test are added together and plotted as above for 'test' scores. The scores on even-numbered items (questions 2, 4, 6, etc) are added together and treated as the 'retest' scores.

Suppose we have an objective test on 'product knowledge' and we use it to estimate the knowledge of 10 of our sales staff. The test has 80 items and each correct item scores one mark. The maximum possible scores are 40 for odd items and 40 for even items. Our 10 staff score as follows:

Candidate	A	B	C	D	E	F	G	H	J	K
Total score	77	76	74	73	69	67	67	54	46	42
Odd items correct	38	39	36	38	33	35	33	24	26	20
Even items correct	39	37	38	35	36	32	34	30	20	22

Totals:	Odd items	322
	Even items	323

Means:	Odd items	32.2
	Even items	32.3

Plot the 10 candidates into the four quadrants

Now calculate the value of $= \dfrac{Q2 \times Q4}{Q1 \times Q3}$

Note: an empty quadrant takes the value of 1 and this avoids the division of a sum by 0 (which would result in infinity).

Is the test sufficiently reliable?

(The worked example is over the page, but it is better to try it for yourself before looking at that.)

Improving reliability

It will never be possible to achieve absolute reliability when testing ability by use of samples. Reliability can be improved by increasing the size of the sample. This means that if the estimated reliability falls below 0.8, more test items need to be written to increase the length of the test and thus the size of the sample of the ability being assessed.

It is also possible to improve reliability by standardising the test conditions – the physical conditions, the instructions, and so on.

A third factor that affects reliability is the marking system. Improvements can usually be made to the scoring system by using trained observers, or subject specialists. The use of detailed marking guides is also recommended.

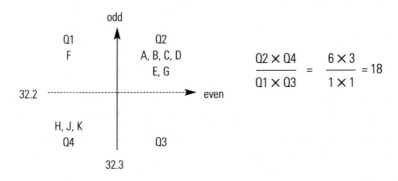

$$\frac{Q2 \times Q4}{Q1 \times Q3} = \frac{6 \times 3}{1 \times 1} = 18$$

Estimated reliability = approx 0.83

B ▪ APPENDIX: APPROACHES TO EVALUATION

In the main part of the book we discussed practical techniques for evaluating changes in effectiveness and behaviour and also the quality and quantity of learning. In this appendix we change the focus to the underlying philosophy of evaluation rather than the techniques. The questions addressed are:

- What sort of process is evaluation?

- What sort of process should it be?

Formulating answers to these questions will identify the kind of information that needs to be collected and the methods by which it should be gathered.

Evaluation, as a professional area of expertise, has developed from attempts to improve the quality of education. The main approach advocated has been influenced by historical and economic factors, and three distinct phases can be identified. Early attempts at evaluation emphasised measurement and testing, assessing whether pupils had learned what might be expected of children of their age. A later development was the introduction of objectives to control the curriculum. Evaluation of a programme could then be made by assessing the extent to which these objectives had been achieved. More recent approaches have acknowledged that views of the strengths and weaknesses of particular programmes will differ. Evaluation following this sort of approach is a process of collecting the views of a sample of interested parties and summarising them. The evaluation report will show what consensus exists and identify where there are significant differences in the opinions of the interested parties.

EVALUATION AS TESTING

Testing people's knowledge and skills is still an important part of learning within the world of work. Assessment of present levels and setting goals for the achievement of higher levels is an important source of motivation to learn. Post-learning examinations and tests are also used to ensure that people can reach a certain set standard, and hence that applicants are qualified in aspects of technical education needed for their work. Success in tests of knowledge and skills is also a criterion required for membership of many professional bodies. The standards against which candidates will be judged are set by committees of experienced members, and the method of assessment will usually also be agreed within this forum. Evaluation is a process of deciding what the standards are, how to test whether candidates have reached them, and making a judgement on each individual candidate. Some of the problems involved in doing this have been discussed in Chapters 4 and 5, and some of the methods that can be used have been described.

Tests may also be used for purposes of comparison. Results may be used to compare the ability of individuals and thus to predict effectiveness. There are some technical problems involved in this. Probably the most serious is that of establishing that the test situation is sufficiently reliable to allow predictions to be made. Appendix A includes a discussion of how to establish test reliability. Tests that are diagnostic in nature (such as 'trainability tests' or 'assessment centre' tasks), may also be used to identify areas of weakness that need correcting by some developmental process.

Evaluation by testing knowledge and skills has a place within an organisational context, but it will rarely be sufficient on its own. Employees will use knowledge and skills to perform tasks in the workplace, and their ability to apply them to work tasks is also important. This suggests setting up the testing situation to reflect, as accurately as is possible, the work situation and this brings us to a second approach to evaluation.

EVALUATION AS MEETING OBJECTIVES

After the First World War, a good deal of experimentation took place in educational establishments. Education was much more widely available and it was recognised that the greater range of abilities within pupils might require different approaches. Evaluation was necessary to compare the value of new and progressive school curricula with more conventional ones. To try to produce some common ground for comparison purposes, it was suggested that the curricula needed to be organized by the use of objectives. Objectives were seen as being crucial because they were the basis for planning, for guiding the instruction, and for the preparation of test and assessment procedures. The process of evaluation proposed (Tyler 1950) had a number of phases:

- Collect, from as wide a consultation as possible, a pool of objectives that might be related to the curriculum.

- Screen the objectives carefully to select a subset that covers the desirable changes.

- Express these objectives in terms of the student behaviours that are expected.

- Develop instruments for testing each objective. These must meet acceptable standards of objectivity, reliability and validity.

- Apply the instruments before and after learning experiences.

- Examine the results to discover strengths and any weaknesses in the curriculum.

- Develop hypotheses about reasons for weaknesses and attempt to rectify these.

- Modify the curriculum and recycle the process.

This sounds a very logical and sensible way of designing an educational system and I have quoted it in full because it also has great relevance to training in organisations. Would that we all had the time and the ability to do this for each of our training programmes!

The educational establishment, at least in the UK, did very little to develop this work into a rationale for school curricula. After the Second World War, further developmental work on the structure of knowledge (Bloom 1956) was also largely ignored by the educational establishment. Indeed, it was only in the 1990s that the UK government started to force this way of thinking on to an unwilling educational establishment by the introduction of the core curriculum.

The use of objectives did, however, strike a chord with those interested in training within organisations. Work on programmed instruction (Mager 1962) led to the development of a behavioural objectives approach for technical education and training. These objectives contain three statements:

1 A performance which is to be demonstrated. This should be an observable behaviour which demonstrates that the candidate can do something; mere understanding is not enough.

2 The conditions under which this performance is to be tested. These conditions should closely resemble those when performing the task in the workplace.

3 The standards that are considered to be acceptable. These should be related to adequate job performance levels.

The trainees are offered these detailed objectives as goals, and evaluation is a matter of assessing how many of them have been attained by individuals and groups. The process has proved to be very successful in improving the effectiveness and efficiency of training. There are three main reasons for this:

- The objectives are simulations of key job tasks. When they are achieved they ensure task mastery, and thus transfer of training.

- The objectives direct the attention of the trainees and allow them to self-set goals, thus building motivation into the learning situation.

- Because the objectives are agreed by a committee rather than by a trainer, and on the basis of careful job analysis rather than out-of-date experience, the resulting training has a very sharp focus on 'need-to-know'. It is therefore much more efficient and usually more effective than 'learn as much as you can'.

There are a number of problems with this approach to controlling and evaluating training.

- The objectives are often difficult to write, and great care is needed to avoid listing what can easily be tested rather than what should be learned.

- The trainers, particularly those who enjoy demonstrating their expertise, may feel that many of the key decisions about how to design and run courses have been removed from them.

- The process clearly identifies where the training is not going well, and this increased level of accountability is difficult for some trainers to accept. (My own view is that this is why this approach has never been accepted within education.)

The approach is still used very successfully in the armed forces, where it was originally developed, and in some other large organisations where there is a good deal of technical, operative training. It has never really been accepted within management training and development, where how people carry out tasks is seen as being less important than how they discharge their responsibilities. Something very like the behavioural objectives approach is now being introduced into many organisations, again under pressure from the UK government, through the use of National Vocational Qualifications (NVQs). These require the demonstration of abilities in a work-related context rather than the teaching and examining of technical skills within a classroom. The way in which the skills are described and the format for testing has clearly been influenced by the work on behavioural objectives.

Part of the reason why this approach has not been more widely accepted is that objectives are being set as tests of the ability to carry out job tasks. Many argue that evaluation should not be just about behaviour, that there are other levels that are of interest. This has led to a number of attempts to specify objectives at a number of levels. The first important contribution, and still the most influential (Kirkpatrick 1959), proposed that objectives should be set for four levels:

1   the *reactions* of the trainees to the programme – what they thought of it

2   measuring the amount of *learning* of principles, facts, skills and attitudes

3   changes in *behaviour* in the job

4   *results:* changes in criteria of organizational effectiveness.

It was pointed out in Chapter 8 that most organisations carry out evaluations at the reactions level; some measure learning in technical training, but few attempt the higher levels (Ralphs and Stephan 1986; HMSO 1989). I hope that the readers of this book will feel more confident in doing this, as how to set objectives at these levels was the subject of Chapters 2 and 3. It is not easy to set objectives at these levels, but it is possible, and it is becoming more and more necessary to do so. The logic of this objectives-based approach is that goals should be set, at each level, before the learning activities are designed. These objectives form the basis for later evaluation, which should establish the extent to which they have been achieved.

The setting of learning objectives is also to be recommended for on-job development and activities other than off-job courses. The developing employee and the supervisor (perhaps assisted by a member of the training department) analyse the possibilities for learning within the tasks to be done over (say) the next six months. A learning contract is then drawn up which specifies some four to six objectives to be achieved during the period. A simple format for such a contract was shown in Table 8.1 (p. 112).

Most trainers, when advising others on how to evaluate training, use some form of setting objectives, usually at the four levels listed above. This is not surprising – deciding what training is intended to achieve, pre-setting objectives to specify what effects should be seen, and then evaluating whether they have been achieved, is a sound way to ensure effective training. In practice, however, it is often difficult to produce clear linkages between training objectives and organisational goals. Given the trend of looking for organisational returns from training investment, this is a serious problem.

An important aspect of this problem is the extent to which the objectives for a programme are shared. If there is a high degree of consensus about what the programme should achieve, objectives-based evaluation should be possible. Experience of using impact analysis (p. 13) suggests that there is often a wide range of views about a programme. For instance, in a study carried out by one of my students, representatives from production, marketing and finance had very different views about an MSc programme in engineering that was being sponsored by a manufacturing organisation. Another example, from the public sector, was the widely different views expressed about the Children's Act and its implications, by residential social workers, social workers involved in fostering, and representatives of the finance function.

What is your view? In your experience, is an organisation *one* group of people with shared goals and common purpose? An alternative view, which recognises the political aspect of organizations, is that organizations are made up of several groups of people, each with different goals. If this is the case, an approach to evaluation that recognises it might be more appropriate than one that assumes shared objectives.

RESPONSIVE EVALUATION

Responsive evaluation (Stake 1975) has been developed over the past 30 years to cope with the situation where the evaluator is less concerned with the stated objectives of the programme than with how it is seen by various interested parties – the 'stakeholders'. These stakeholders will usually fall into three broad classes:

- *agents* who run or use the programme that is to be evaluated

- *beneficiaries* who profit in some way from the use of the programme

- *victims* who suffer in some way because of the programme (Guba and Lincoln 1989).

For a training programme, these are likely to be: the staff organising the programme, those delivering it, and a sample of those who will be affected by it (participants, their supervisors and more senior line managers).

The evaluator will talk to these stakeholders and ask them what they have to say about the programme that is positive (their *claims*), and what *concerns* they have about it. It helps in this if the evaluator has first of all observed a run of the programme and has some feel for what it is trying to do and how it is trying to do it. Different stakeholders will often have different claims and concerns, and the function of the evaluator is to identify these and then produce a report that shows:

- what consensus there is about the programme

- what issues there are about which people disagree.

This report is circulated to representatives of the main stakeholder groups, who then become aware of the claims and concerns of others. The issues that have been identified will probably need further investigation to discover if they are due to lack of information or some deeper cause.

The circulation of this interim report will affect the way in which the stakeholders think about the programme. It is thus an intervention in its own right, and the evaluator has become part of the process rather than an observer of it. Usually there is a second phase of planning further evaluation to satisfy the various issues and concerns. The direction of the evaluation is thus not fixed at the outset, but readjusted as data become available.

My experience of using this kind of evaluative process is that line managers welcome being involved and value the opportunity to express their views. They are often impressed that trainers should talk to them in this way and they usually become more sympathetic to training initiatives generally, whether or not they value the particular programme under discussion.

The underlying philosophy of responsive evaluation is very different from that of following up objectives. It does not set out to discover the 'truth' of whatever has been achieved by the training programme. Rather, it sets out to 'construct' the truth as seen from a number of different perspectives. It is not part of the strict scientific approach, where causes are sought. It is an example of action research in which the interested parties collect the data, make some sense of it, and then decide what to do next.

The strength of responsive evaluation is that it is a collaboration between the evaluator and the key stakeholders, and it takes into account different perspectives. Where organisations are trying to use training programmes as a part of a change process, this will be necessary in order to tailor the intervention to the needs of the various subgroups. Change implies influencing people, and a powerful method of achieving this is to consult and involve them. If, as some would argue, the nature of organisational change is essentially political, an evaluative approach that recognises this political dimension should be more appropriate than one that does not.

REFERENCES AND FURTHER READING

BLOOM B.S. (1956) *Taxonomy of Educational Objectives: Cognitive Domain*. London, Longmans.

GUBA E.G. *and* LINCOLN Y.S. (1989) *Fourth Generation Evaluation*. Beverly Hills, Calif, Sage.

HMSO (1989) *Training in Britain: A study of funding, activity and attitudes*. London, HMSO.

KIRKPATRICK D.L. (1959) 'Techniques for evaluating training programmes'. *Journal of the American Society of Training Directors*. 13, 3–9 and 21–26; 14, 13–18 and 28–32.

MAGER R.F. (1962) *Preparing Objectives for Programmed Instruction*. San Francisco, Fearon.

RALPHS L.T. *and* STEPHAN E. (1986) 'HRD in the Fortune 500'. *Training and Development Journal.* 40, 69–76.

STAKE R.E. (ed) (1975) *Evaluating the Arts in Education: A responsive approach.* Columbus, Ohio, Merrill.

TYLER R.W. (1950) *Basic Principles of Curriculum and Instruction Design.* Chicago, University of Chicago Press.

INDEX